VINTAGE HUMOUR

Vintage Humour

The Islamic Wine Poetry of Abu Nuwas

ALEX ROWELL

HURST & COMPANY, LONDON

First published in English in the United Kingdom in 2017 by
C. Hurst & Co. (Publishers) Ltd.,
41 Great Russell Street, London, WC1B 3PL

Printed in the United Kingdom by Bell & Bain Ltd, Glasgow

A Cataloguing-in-Publication data record for this book is available from the British Library.

ISBN: 9781849048972

www.hurstpublishers.com

Distributed in the United States, Canada and Latin America by
Oxford University Press, 198 Madison Avenue, New York,
NY 10016,United States of America.

To the writers, drinkers, and freethinkers of the Arab and Islamic worlds, long may they live.

Contents

Introduction

When news of Abu Nuwas' death (c. 814 AD) reached the reigning caliph, 'Abd Allah ibn Harun al-Ma'mun, the emperor styled as the Commander of the Believers is said to have cried out, 'The charm of our time has departed [...] Allah's curse upon whoever disparages him!'[1]

If it seems odd in retrospect that the supreme authority of the Muslim world should have so lamented the passing of a notorious inebriate, an unabashed bisexual, and an internationally scandalous satirist of religious and cultural conservatism, it is only one in a long line of contradictions and ironies surrounding the poet generally agreed to have written the best wine poetry in the Arabic language, and some of its finest verse of any kind, full stop.

To Arabic readers, the man whose poems remain widely loved or reviled (but in either case read) more than 1,200 years on from his demise needs little introduction. To the Anglophone world, however, this Muslim Rochester or Wilde continues to be almost entirely unknown, save for the crude caricature taking his name in the *One Thousand and One Nights* folk tales. 'I have found that there is little in the

English language or for a matter of fact in any European language about a man who is eminently worth knowing', wrote W.H. Ingrams in his 1933 *Abu Nuwas in Life and in Legend*.[2] It would be difficult to argue much has changed in the intervening eighty-four years.

In which case, before getting into the qualities that make the man so eminently worth knowing – the comic genius, the lyric virtuosity, the striking humanism, for a start – it may be useful to begin with a quick biographical gloss,[3] which will also necessarily touch on the history of one of human civilisation's truly transformational times.

Al-Hasan ibn Hani', who would grow up to be nicknamed 'Abu Nuwas' ('He of the dangling hair-lock'), was born in the late 750s AD – probably 757 or 758[4] – in the village of Istanah Atar near the city of Ahwaz, in modern-day Iran.[5] This was an extraordinarily tumultuous, as well as propitious, moment for a future writer to be born, being less than a decade after Islam's first dynasty (that of the Umayyads, ruling from Damascus) was overthrown by the rebels known as the 'Abbasids, who would build their own imposing capital from scratch over a – then-insignificant – site on the banks of the River Tigris called Baghdad.

Al-Hasan's father, Hani', affiliated with the Yemeni al-Hakam tribe, had been a soldier in the army of the last Umayyad caliph, Marwan ibn Muhammad, until the 'Abbasid victory in 750 returned him to his Persian wife, Julluban, in Ahwaz. The penurious newlyweds lived a laborious existence; Hani' as shepherd and weaver, Julluban as a maker of saddlebags, socks, and possibly bamboo products. Along with al-Hasan, they are said to have had a daughter and two other sons.

Not long after al-Hasan's birth, the family moved southwest to Basra, the nearest major city in what was known (even then) as Iraq. Hani' would soon die – for reasons that remain obscure – leaving Julluban to raise the children alone on the fruits of her artisanry. When he was old enough, al-Hasan was sent to the mosque to receive the conventional instruction in reading, writing, and Qur'an recitation.

To grow up in Basra at that time was – difficult as many may, regrettably, find it to imagine now – to grow up in an exhilarating intellectual, cultural, and socioeconomic hub. As the proud hometown of venerable philosophers, grammarians, and theologians, Basra enjoyed an academic rivalry with its northwestern neighbour, Kufa, analogous to that between Oxford and Cambridge today. Commercially, as a key maritime port, 'it was a centre between Syria and Persia, its trade extending eastward to India and China, and westward to the farthest Western countries.'[6] Its streets and squares were 'a meeting place of every creed and sect, descended upon [...] by Zoroastrians, and *zindeeqs*,[7] and the people of India and China with all their various customs and rites and requirements in times of both seriousness and levity.'[8] Politically, the whole of Iraq was still rapt with the revolutionary fervour that had just toppled the Umayyads, and the ʿAbbasid newcomers quickly faced challenges from the ultra-fanatical Khawarij[9] and the factions that would develop into what we now know as the Shiʿa,[10] inter alia. In 762, when al-Hasan would have been four or five, a rebellion led by the ʿAlid[11] leader al-Nafs al-Zakiyya ('The Pure Soul') briefly succeeded in seizing Basra and Ahwaz before ultimately being crushed by the Caliph al-Mansur, whose men carried out gruesome reprisals on purported ʿAlid sympathisers in the aftermath.

Perhaps most pertinently for the future bacchic bard, Basra was also a distinguished nightlife venue; 'one of the great metropolises of indulgence, teeming with places of entertainment and outlets of pleasure and causes of temptation and sin.'[12] Before very long at all, al-Hasan would be joining the city's literati on their nocturnal tours of the taverns, making the intimate acquaintance of the waiters, singers, and vintners whom he would later portray so vividly in his verse.

First, though, he needed to learn the craft, which by all accounts he did with staggering precocity. His first teacher, Yaʿqub al-Hadhrami, is quoted as telling the young boy who had quickly memorised the Qur'an that he was 'the best Qur'an reciter in Basra.'[13] After that, Julluban sent him to work in the perfume souk to sharpen incense sticks, a chore from which he escaped at every available opportunity to the mosque, which functioned in between prayer times as a kind of university lecture hall, even a social club. Here he would receive an education from some of Basra's leading scholars in the Islamic domains of Qur'an, Hadith,[14] and jurisprudence, as well as the more secular disciplines of grammar, astronomy, the history and lineages of the old Arab tribes, and, of course, classical poetry.

He was at this time 'handsome-faced, fine-coloured, white and soft of body, slender, with a large head and dangling side-locks, a rhotacism on the letter "R" so as to make it a "gh", and a constant huskiness in his throat'.[15] He drew attention in the mosque for his looks and also 'his combination of light-spiritedness and liveliness with intelligence and learning power'.[16]

His break, however, would in fact come at the perfume souk, when one of Kufa's poetic celebrities, Waliba ibn al-Hubab, chanced to buy some incense sticks from his stall. Striking up a conversation with the youth, Waliba was impressed by his quick wit and knowledge, and offered to mentor him in poetry. Realising who he was, a stunned al-Hasan recited one of his couplets, saying he'd hoped to travel to Kufa expressly to meet him one day. Waliba's response was to propose he accompany him back to Kufa straight away. With Julluban having by now remarried and abandoned her son to the perfumists, he didn't hesitate to accept.

Under Waliba's wing, in Kufa the teenage[17] al-Hasan would take the first tangible strides of his poetic career. Yet Waliba's most enduring influence on him would have less to do with formal didactics than initiations of another kind. For as well as being the peer of Basra in learning, Kufa was every bit its equal in conviviality, and Waliba was among its foremost merrymakers. Introducing al-Hasan to a clique of literary debauchees (Hammad 'Ajrad, Mutee' ibn Iyas, and Yahya ibn Ziyad, inter alia), he had the adolescent drinking wine 'before the hair had sprouted on his upper lip'.[18] Together they would spend their evenings (and often their mornings) carousing with the city's famous songstresses – often capable poets themselves, and who, like the young men pouring the glasses, were typically slaves – or picnicking in the verdant fields on the outskirts of town. It was in this company that al-Hasan is said to have uttered his first poetic composition, during a literary game in which the poets took turns outdoing one another in improvisation.[19] More would soon follow, and, for all the revelry, Waliba grasped that the young man's talent was exceptional, even unique. Thus did he arrange, at al-Hasan's request, for him to spend a year in the desert with the Bedouin to absorb their renowned linguistic purity and peculiar vocabulary.

Armed with a now-dazzling lexicon, upon his return from the desert al-Hasan made for Basra to polish his art further still. This he did under the tutelage of a second, and very different kind of mentor, the esteemed literary scholar and poet Khalaf al-Ahmar, whose austere rigour made the ideal complement to Waliba's decidedly more informal approach. 'Khalaf was a philological master of the great tradition of ancient Bedouin poetry and had both the authority and innate skill to round Abu Nuwas' poetic education'.[20] A popular legend has it that Khalaf refused to allow his disciple to compose anything before he had memorised 1,000 poems from the classical canon. When al-Hasan duly recited them all flawlessly from memory a few days later, his tutor then demanded he forget every one of them. Only after that monumental feat was he permitted to start writing. While clearly an exaggeration, there is no disputing Abu Nuwas' mastery of the pre-Islamic oeuvre, to which allusions (often but not always satirical) abound in his poetry, adding a layer of depth and sophistication for which he largely had Khalaf to thank.

As he matured as a writer, he also experienced another formative – indeed perhaps pivotal – development: he fell in love. Janan was a slave owned by the notable Thaqeef clan in Basra. By all accounts exceptionally beautiful, she was also 'refined, elegant, intelligent, and knowledgeable about history and poetry'.[21] Spotting her one day while reciting verse at a gathering, he was instantly besotted, and set about pursuing her with an obsessive single-mindedness over the course of many weeks. Their personalities were clearly ill-matched – she's described as 'staid, upright, chaste, timid, untalkative',[22] and from the beginning she distrusted the intentions of the hellraising, omnisexual hedonist.

Nonetheless, al-Hasan persisted undeterred, following her everywhere and missing no occasion to remind her of his infatuation. Seeing her one day at a funeral, he arranged for a messenger to send her a letter bearing the words:

O, moon sighted at a funeral
Mourning in grief among cognates
Crying, dispersing pearls[23] from a jonquil
And beating[24] a rose with red dates
Weep not for the one dead in his grave
But for the one you killed by the gate[25]

Eventually, after another few dozen epistolary tributes of this kind, Janan began to warm to him, and permitted him to visit her. Their most physical of encounters occurred, improbably enough, while she was in Mecca on the Hajj pilgrimage. Learning of her travel plans in advance, the poet set out independently to make the same journey. At the moment she leant in for the ritual kiss of the Black Stone in the corner of the Ka'ba, he thrust his own face in next to hers, so that their cheeks met. As he would later boast:

We stayed, concealed by our hands
Placed at the sides of our faces
Doing, in the Mosque, that which
The pious don't do in such places[26]

It wasn't, however, to last, in part because Janan's masters (the joyless philistine and miser Muhammad ibn Khalid and his wife 'Ammara) did everything to encourage her doubts about his character, convinced he was an irredeemable lecher and queer stringing her along as some kind of elaborate joke. The end came when the family moved her away to a relative's house outside the city.

It's said that Abu Nuwas (as he was now known, having been given the cognomen by Khalaf al-Ahmar)[27] never loved another woman again, and commentators have understandably been tempted to invest the Janan episode with no end of psychological significance. While Sidqi is probably overstating the case in the following, it's hard to imagine there isn't some truth to it, and that the abandon with which the poet subsequently threw himself into libertinism, and his lifelong contempt for moral pontificators and prohibitionists, were at the very least stiffened by the experience:

> There's no doubt that Abu Nuwas was truly prepared to correct his situation and straighten his character and right his conduct and be sound in his religion, if his relationship with Janan, in her reason and full refinement, had lasted, and led to its natural result of him marrying the woman he loved.[28]

Indeed, it's arresting to think what a loss for world literature it might have been had he in fact settled down in the Basra suburbs and become a wholesome family man. Fortunately for us (if not necessarily for him) that wasn't to be, and instead the heartbroken poet set off – after an almighty drinking binge in Kufa and a series of nearby Christian monasteries – for the capital whose name he would help engrave ineffaceably in history, and that would make his own *nom de guerre* imperishable in turn.

One can scarcely overstate how astonishing the new city of Baghdad – completed in 766 – would have appeared to those then seeing it for the first time. Its circular outer wall, sixty feet tall and four miles in circumference, was topped by a 105-ft.-high inner wall, inside of which were markets and houses, and, after a third wall, the royal precinct, with its numerous palaces, barracks, and administrative offices. At the very centre stood the caliph's 360,000 sq. ft. Golden Gate Palace, capped with its 130-ft. green dome, 'visible for miles around',[29] next to the 90,000 sq. ft. Great Mosque. By the time of Abu Nuwas' arrival in the late 780s, the city had also sprawled considerably outside the original walls, spilling east over the Tigris, where some of its finest buildings were located. In its colossal size and opulence, it was a global metropolis almost without equal; in the words of the late historian Philip K. Hitti, its 'prestige and splendour [were] unrivalled in the Middle Ages, except perhaps by Constantinople'.[30]

Though he could hardly have known it at the time, Abu Nuwas was destined to see the city at the very crest of its glory. His advent is said to have approximately coincided with the start, in 786, of the twenty-three-year reign of Harun al-Rashid, the caliph whose very name endures to this day as a byword for the Islamic Golden Age. 'History and legend unite in placing the most brilliant period of Baghdad during the caliphate of Harun al-Rashid', writes Hitti.[31] Master of the Muslim world, Harun would also chastise Christendom by imposing 'an ignominious tax' on the Byzantine Emperor Nicephorus I; 'marking the topmost point ever reached by Abbasid power'.[32] By the turn of the ninth century, there were 'two imperial names standing supreme in world affairs: Charlemagne in the West and Harun al-Rashid in the East. Of the two Harun was undoubtedly the more powerful and represented the higher culture'.[33]

Indeed, the might of Harun's Baghdad was much more than merely military or monetary. Invigorating the process initiated by his grandfather al-Mansur, the young caliph oversaw an industrial-scale wave of translation into Arabic of Greek, Persian, Syriac, and Sanskrit classics of both the sciences and humanities. Aristotle's philosophy, Euclid's mathematics, Ptolemy's astronomy – these and countless other magnum opuses were rendered into Arabic under either Harun or his son, al-Ma'mun, whose name in particular is associated with a quasi-academy known as the House of Wisdom.[34] 'All this', as Hitti writes, 'while Europe was almost totally ignorant of Greek thought or science. For while al-Rashid and al-Ma'mun were delving into Greek and Persian philosophy their contemporaries in the West, Charlemagne and his lords, were reportedly dabbling in the art of writing their names.'[35]

These translations, invaluable though they were in their own right (not least because many of the Greek and other originals have since been lost), would more importantly galvanise later 'Abbasid generations whose brightest minds would add to and improve on their non-Arab forefathers, turning Baghdad into an Enlightenment centre unsurpassed for more than five centuries – until the first stirrings of the European Renaissance (which itself owed no small debt to the percolations of 'Abbasid knowledge via Sicily and Andalusia). Al-Battani (a.k.a. Albategnius, d. 929), for example, 'made several emendations to Ptolemy and rectified the calculations for the orbits of the moon and certain planets',[36] earning the stated admiration of Copernicus and Galileo half a millennium later. 'Umar al-Khayyam (d. 1131), perhaps best known for his own impious and bibulous poetry, the *Ruba'iyyat*,[37] would also help produce a calendar more accurate than the Gregorian[38] and make substantial advances on the pioneering algebra of his predecessor, al-Khawarizmi (d. 850), from whose name came the English word 'algorithm'.[39] The medical encyclopaedia of the polymath Ibn Sina (a.k.a. Avicenna, d. 1037) would remain 'the chief guide to medical science in the West'[40] until the seventeenth century. Countless other influential works were produced on everything from chemistry to philosophy to geography to music. Harun's ultimate legacy, in sum, was to have set in motion 'the most momentous intellectual awakening in the history of Islam and one of the most significant in the whole history of thought and culture'.[41]

Abu Nuwas would witness, and eventually make his own contribution to the birth of this awakening, though initially from a distance. Whatever standing he'd managed to accrue in Basra and Kufa mattered little at the imperial court of the Commander of the Believers in Baghdad. To so much as gain the opportunity to have his poetry heard by the caliph, he would have to work his way up the lesser functionaries of government, most conspicuously the powerful clan of Persian administrators known as the Barmakids.

In this he had little success. Attempting to win the Barmakids' favour by the conventional ruse of writing a panegyric in their praise, he was indignant to receive only a pittance in reward.[42] His impetuous response was to skewer their hugely influential vizier, Ja'far, in a lampoon, attaining revenge but making an enemy of the man who would remain Harun's closest aide until 803, when the caliph's abrupt decision to quash the Barmakids' influence led to his brutal murder.

The poet's fortunes would improve somewhat under Ja'far's successor as vizier, al-Fadhl ibn al-Rabee', though it remains a curious fact that – very much contrary to the picture painted in the (wholly unreliable) *One Thousand and One Nights* – Abu Nuwas never managed to get on especially close terms with Harun.[43] This wasn't only due to the Barmakid matter. While certainly appreciative of literature, and by no means averse to a drink in private,[44] Harun was on the whole a much more temperate, conservative character than Abu Nuwas; gravely serious about religious matters; with little tolerance for the poet's irreverent and ribald sides. Indeed, he would have Abu Nuwas jailed on several occasions, for transgressions ranging from drunkenness to blasphemy[45] to a satire against the northern Arab tribes (with whom Harun, as a Hashemite, was affiliated).

Out of luck at the caliph's court, the poet would have to rely on lesser patrons for his livelihood, the most prominent of whom were the Nawbakhts, a scholarly Persian family whose members included Harun's court astrologer and librarian, Abu Sahl. While it may be that Abu Nuwas' golden years would only come after Harun's death in 809, the two decades he spent in Baghdad prior to that must still have been illustrious enough in their own way. He earned the esteem and friendship of the capital's established literary heavyweights, many of whom – Abu al-ʿAtahiya and Muslim ibn al-Walid, for instance – are themselves still widely read in Arabic today. He drank prodigiously at the taverns of the city and its surrounding towns. And while it's not often possible to date individual poems with much precision, it can be said with confidence that many of the surviving works were written during the Harun years.[46]

Nonetheless, it was a sign of his enduring difficulties under al-Rashid that toward the end of the caliph's reign – perhaps in need of money, or in fear of the increasingly irascible sovereign's wrath, or both – Abu Nuwas moved to Egypt, taking up residence under the patronage of the regional tax collector, al-Khaseeb.[47] Here, in the principal Muslim town of Fustat (Cairo would not be built for another 160 years) his panegyrics were received warmly, as were – if one of Abu Hiffan's more vibrant stories is to be believed – his advances on certain local Christian gentlemen.[48] He's said to have liked the Egyptian weather but to have been terrified of the Nile's crocodiles, and to have 'hated' such beverages as were on offer.[49] When al-Khaseeb lost his post in 806/7, about a year after Abu Nuwas' arrival, the poet began his return to Baghdad, passing by the superior vintners of Syria's Homs (including a Jew named Levi) and Iraq's ʿAna and Qutrabbul in a determined rampage amusingly recounted in the poem I SOUGHT PLEASURE IN QUTRABBUL.

Saddled with insurrections on the fringes of the empire; renewed hostilities with the Byzantines; the (self-inflicted) loss of the highly capable Barmakids; and deteriorating health to boot, Harun was in less humorous spirits than ever by the time Abu Nuwas arrived back in town. It wasn't long before the poet wound up once again in prison, where he might well have spent the rest of his life were it not for Harun's fateful decision to travel to the eastern Khorasan province[50] in 808 to confront the revolt of Rafiʿ ibn Laith, scion of the Umayyad *ancien régime*. Harun would die of illness there, near the city of Toos, in March 809, leaving his son Muhammad al-Amin to succeed him in Baghdad.

A more fortuitous turn of events for the poet could scarcely have been imagined. The new twenty-one-year-old caliph had an outstanding appetite for Baghdad's Dionysian attractions, and where his father had seen in Abu Nuwas a deviant and degenerate, the son saw an obvious kindred spirit. The pair, indeed, are said to have befriended one another even before Harun's death.[51] In any case, one of al-Amin's first acts after taking the throne was to have the poet released and summoned for a session of poetry and wine.[52] 'There could be no more suitable drinking partner for a caliph', al-Amin is recorded as saying, 'than one of [Abu Nuwas'] refinement, and charm, and knowledge'.[53] Now in his early fifties, the poet was at last to have his day in court.

It was an opportunity of which he would make maximum use. In the sunlight of his newfound freedom, his artistic flower would reach its brightest bloom – as its satirical prickles would turn their sharpest. A poem like IT WAS EVENING, AND HE WAS SOBER shows starkly how creative – and daring – Abu Nuwas was encouraged to become under his new patron/partner-in-crime; in a flippant parody of the conventional panegyric, he praises the caliph not for his regal grandeur or martial virility but for his singular excellence as drinking companion:

They squinted, astonished, at the drinks partner
　　For it was evening, and he was sober
Only one attempt is necessary
　　To waken him from drunken slumber

And he doesn't say, 'No! Leave me'
Or ask, 'What is it you're after?'
But rather, 'Pour me', adding too:
'Make it straight if you've no water'
When noon strikes, he goes to pray
Though he skips afternoon and night prayer
Those he prays at the other's time
Always completing what's required
That's Muhammad, I offer him my soul
As he deserves – and how paltry's the offer

Drenched in booze as it was, their relationship was clearly literary no less than libationary. Abu Hiffan recounts a story of the caliph betting his favourite poet a thousand dinars[54] he couldn't write a stanza rhyming on the near-impossible '*khakha*' letters (he did, producing no fewer than five lines).[55] Their other common interests encompassed everything from music to hunting to the polo-like sport of *al-sawlajan* (typical of al-Amin's approach to governance was his ordering the construction of a field for this on day two of his reign).[56] Perhaps most controversially, the two shared a taste for a vogue that emerged at al-Amin's saturnalian gatherings; that of female entertainers dressed up as males, in whose honour Abu Nuwas would pioneer a new sub-genre of amorous verse.

They were, in Wagner's words, the poet's 'most brilliant years',[57] in which he wrote a great number of the surviving wine odes. Yet the personal qualities that made al-Amin such vivacious evening company were rather less conducive to the business of high statecraft (he's said to have enjoyed 'setting fire to tax records assembled for his inspection',[58] for example), and it didn't take very long for politics to get in the way of all the fun. Allowing himself to be manipulated by self-interested advisers, al-Amin provoked (or exacerbated)[59] a dispute with his half-brother, al-Ma'mun, whom Harun had designated governor of Khorasan and heir to al-Amin's throne in a pact agreed and signed publicly by all parties while on pilgrimage in Mecca back in 802. As fraternal relations soured, and al-Ma'mun's partisans sought to tarnish the caliph's character, his friendship with Abu Nuwas became one of their explicit angles of attack.[60] This compelled al-Amin to publicly admonish the poet for a time, and even jail him; acts which elicited theatrical declarations of repentance and abstinence in such poems as I DON'T TASTE THE WINE EXCEPT BY NOSE, the comic tone of which raises doubts as to its sincerity.

Al-Amin's problems were soon greater than an inebriated poet, however. By late 810, the strategically vital province of Khorasan (where the 'Abbasid revolution began around sixty years previously) was in open rebellion against Baghdad, led by al-Ma'mun, who had also succumbed to unscrupulous aides pushing for escalation. Al-Amin formally repudiated al-Ma'mun's status as heir apparent, in violation of his late father's wishes and his own word, and sent a large army to depose his brother at the start of 811. In the event, it suffered a surprising and embarrassing defeat in the Persian city of Rayy at the hands of al-Ma'mun's general, Tahir ibn al-Husayn. Sibling rivalry now gave way to full-blown civil war, with each brother's loyalists fighting one another as far away as Syria, the Hijaz, and Egypt. From Khorasan Tahir's invigorated forces moved west into Iraq, quickly sweeping the southern cities and laying siege to Baghdad itself in August 812. For thirteen months the capital's starving and woefully outgunned residents withstood devastating torrents of catapult bombardment; countless men, women, and children perishing as the city's architectural jewels were steadily annihilated:

> Tahir [...] began the systematic demolition of houses in the areas where resistance was fiercest [...] What he did not destroy was ruined by the defenders. The city became a sort of medieval Stalingrad, and a vast swathe of the town to the north and west of the Round City was laid waste. Amin began to raise money by selling off the materials of his palaces; the gilded ceilings and wooden roofs were all destroyed by him or burned by Tahir.[61]

Finally, with the city in rubble, and al-Amin's fighters almost all dead or deserted, Tahir's men prevailed in September 813, capturing and killing the caliph.[62]

This was a terrible outcome for Abu Nuwas, who lost not only his greatest patron but one of his closest friends. An idea of the grief and despondency he underwent in the aftermath is given by the following lines from his elegy for al-Amin:

For him alone did I fear death
Now there's nothing I'm afraid of
Those I don't love fill up the houses
And the graves fill with those I love[63]

He would himself enter the grave within the next two years, seemingly felled by an unspecified illness with probable alcoholic complications.[64] In his last days he grew weak and emaciated, unable to leave the house, but mentally dashing as ever; dealing with the situation as he would any other – that is, with humour and literature:

A dead man's verse comes to you, spoken by
One now stuck between life and demise
Time has wasted his body away, until
He's almost disappeared from Time's eyes
Were you to study my face, there's not
One letter in its book you'd recognise[65]

The end came in what was most likely 814 or 815, when he was generally agreed to have been fifty-seven (fifty-nine in Islamic years). His effects, found in his bedroom by friends after his funeral, are said to have included scraps of paper bearing scrawlings of poetry, sets of backgammon and chess, and an 'oud and tanbur.[66] He was buried in Baghdad at the Shuniziyya cemetery on a hill by the banks of the 'Isa canal known as Tall al-Yahud ('The Hill of the Jews'). He left behind a daughter, Barra, of unknown maternity,[67] and an estranged ex-wife, whom he's said to have divorced immediately after marrying.[68]

Having beheld Baghdad at its most magnificent, during the siege and civil war that engulfed his final years Abu Nuwas also saw much of his beloved city obliterated, in the first of a series of calamities that would lead ultimately to the fall of the 'Abbasid dynasty. Though Baghdad would soon be mostly rebuilt, 'the Golden Gate Palace in the Round City was never lived in by a caliph again',[69] while the magnificent riverside Palace of Eternity, which seems to have actually been preferred by the caliphs as a residence, was also destroyed. Outside the capital, the wider empire never fully recovered from the chaos of the war, which in fact continued for years after al-Amin's death, nearly costing al-Ma'mun himself the caliphate. By 819, when al-Ma'mun finally left Khorasan and arrived in Baghdad, he'd managed to pacify Iraq but 'many areas, including all of Syria, Palestine and Egypt remained outside the control of the government',[70] and would take the best part of the next decade to recoup. Other provinces were lost forever; indeed, crucial to the unique prestige that attaches to Harun's reign is that it was 'the last period when all the central Islamic lands from Ifriqiya [modern Tunisia, Algeria, and Libya] in the west to Sind [modern Pakistan] in the east were under the control of the caliph'.[71] While Abu Nuwas' genius would probably have won him literary immortality no matter when he had happened to be alive, it certainly doesn't detract from his lustre that he had the distinction of being that era's master poet; the star of Islam's most dazzling moment.

At this juncture, the reader may feel rather much has been said about the poet with comparatively little put forward about the poems themselves. By what right does this alcoholic philanderer and jailbird get called a 'genius'? What did he even write about, apart from himself?

A great deal, as it happens. Most poets would, one suspects, be content with becoming the acknowledged laureate of just one genre of the art. Abu Nuwas, however, is credited with having 'perfected'[72] two of them (the wine poem, or *khamriyya*, and the hunting ode, or *tardiyya*), and the more than 1,500 poems in his *Diwan* (collected works) further encompass everything from amorous verse (*ghazal*; sub-divided into *mu'annathat* for female lovers and *mudhakkarat* for males) to lampoons (*hija'*) to panegyrics (*mada'ih*) to ribaldry (*mujoon*) to pious odes (*zuhdiyyat*) to so-called infidel verse (*kufriyyat*). Several of these – most notably the wine, hunting, ribald, and male love categories – were only recognised as fully independent standalone genres after Abu Nuwas did so much to develop and refine their structure and variety.[73] He excelled at everything to which he turned his pen; so much so that the dean of the pious *zuhdiyyat* (of all genres), Abu al-'Atahiya, is said to have begged him not to write any such odes, fearing he'd outshine him.[74] Thus, while he's popularly known in the Arab world today as merely 'the Wine Poet', in fact Abu Nuwas was the early Islamic period's most accomplished and influential poet of any kind, compared by medieval critics to the pre-Islamic master Imru' al-Qays[75] and ranked by some in later centuries above the titan al-Mutanabbi.[76]

This book nonetheless focuses on the wine poems, the *khamriyyat*, the poet's most famous and in many respects most fascinating.[77] By turns lyrical, satirical, frivolous, political, erotic, comic, and philosophical, they draw in fact from all the other elements of his work and can be thought of as the synthesis and culmination of his artistic achievement. What follows is an informal introduction to their principal forms, themes, motifs, and running jokes.[78]

At their most fundamental, the poems are simply and literally about wine; exalted descriptions of its appearance, fragrance, taste, and effects on mind, body, and soul. The wine might be a rubicund burgundy, like 'clear agate', or perhaps 'yellow as purest gold'. When mixed with water – a practice shared with the ancient Greeks, and recommended in the Babylonian Talmud[79] – it would fizz with bubbles like 'pearls', glowing as brightly as coal or a lantern, illuminating the faces of drinkers under the night sky. Its perfume might be of a carnation bouquet, or 'musk, with a hint of apple'. When in a lyrical mood, there was really no end to the images the poet could dream up for his potations: one wine's glistening surface is likened to a wobbling tear held back between the eyelids of a lover concealing a secret longing.

The best wine, then as now, was aged for many years; buried away in a vintner's cellar until its clay cask was smothered in cobwebs. Some of Abu Nuwas' wines were very old indeed – known to a pre-Islamic Persian king, or a Roman Caesar, or the ancient Thamud people, or even Noah (who made sure to stow it safely on his Ark). One particularly special wine was in fact 'preserved for Adam before his creation'. Another, slightly younger, draught recalls making the acquaintance of Moses and Alexander the Great.

These wines were savoured in a variety of settings, from floral riverside meadows to Christian monasteries to the caliph's palaces. Very often they were enjoyed in taverns, typically run by Persian, Christian, or Jewish proprietors. Ideally, they would be served in gilded or gemstone vessels, intricately engraved on their bases and sides with depictions of horsemen bounding off to hunt or battle (a sheepskin pouch would have to suffice on less glamorous occasions). If it was a quality establishment, these vessels would be filled from glass carafes poured by young men or women (it might not be easy to tell which), with 'earlocks curled like scorpions' tails', sensual 'swaggers', and languid eyelids like a 'slumbering gazelle's'. If it was a real party, there would also be music; an 'oud providing the backing for a singer, usually female, who would reel off renditions of popular poems till the sun came up.

Almost every *khamriyya*, by definition, includes a section chronicling such festivities and the particular wines that accompanied them. Here the poet would draw on a dizzyingly expansive vocabulary, encompassing well over twenty distinct words for 'wine'[80] (try thinking of even three in English) and at least ten for 'cup'. This specialist lexicon further included specific verbs for drinking in the evening (*al-ightibaq*), in the morning (*al-istibah*), and as early as possible (*al-mubakara*). The 'Abbasids, plainly, were no mere 'social' drinkers – one wine synonym, *al-qarqaf*, refers to the 'tremor' experienced when the consumer eventually sobers up.

Yet, naturally, mere description is only one of many elements to the poems, which would hardly be as interesting as they are (or as numerous; the *Diwan* contains over 300) if they were simply accounts of jovial occasions. The point bears repeating that Abu Nuwas was a man of prodigious literary learning, and the originality of his verse consisted not just in its subject matter but in the ingenious games it played with the established poetic tradition. Among his favourite of these was the subversion of one of the oldest and most hallowed conventions in the canon.

From the very earliest surviving pre-Islamic verse onward, a staple of classical Arabic poetry had been the tearful lamenting of the traces (*atlal*) remaining in the desert sands of a former lover's long-abandoned campsite.[81] Poets would describe alighting from their camels at the sight of ash or other debris, weeping in heartache and imploring the remnants to tell them where their lovers had gone, as their friends tried to console them. Beyond this initially amorous association, by the time of 'Abbasid Baghdad the somewhat anachronistic *atlal* topos had come to represent nostalgic glorification of the old Bedouin life, the *illud tempus*, with its pastoral austerity, nomadic grazing, and tribal values – everything, in other words, that Abu Nuwas and his fellow metropolitan rakes regarded with horror and derision.

As such, the poet developed something of a signature opener, in which he mocked what he portrayed as the benighted and sentimental desert fools sobbing over worthless, primitive rubbish, urging his audience to devote themselves instead to the finer pursuits of drink and free love in the city:

Leave the traces, give them no thought
    Truly, but woe, they bring nothing
And drink wine, though it's forbidden
    For your world's a fleeting dwelling

Or, as another begins:

Nicer than a campsite in Dhu Qar[82]
    Is a vintner's tavern in Anbar[83]
And the smell of sweet basil, and narcissi
    Is finer than saddled camels, by far
And intimacy with gentle maidens
    And a young gazelle wrapped in *zunnar*[84]

Are more pleasant than a tiring desert
And the mirage's cruel canard

At its most elevated, this became a deadpan parody of the original motif, in which the poet affects to weep in mourning at the loss of a beloved tavern:

A drinking house, neglected and abandoned
Traces of past life still marked
Grooves of wine pouches dragged on its soil
And basil bouquets, some moist, some parched

It may not seem outrageously rebellious, but it was enough to earn the rebuke of al-Amin, who – apparently under pressure from conservative tribal types[85] – compelled Abu Nuwas for a time to stop ridiculing the *atlal* trope, saying he had 'done enough damage' (as the poet recounts in I HEAR YOU, LEADER OF THE BELIEVERS, AND OBEY).

More scandalous were his satirical strikes at Islam, which in many ways still read as arrestingly audacious and subversive today as they must have at the time. The mosque – both in the literal sense of the prayer hall and the broader sense of the religious establishment – was a natural impediment to the poet's joie de vivre, and thus had to be lampooned like any other. Very little, evidently, was sacred – everything from distinguished clergymen to the daily prayers to the Ramadan fast to mandatory almsgiving (*zakat*) to the Mecca pilgrimage (four of the five so-called 'pillars' of the faith) was fair game. The following lines are broadly representative:

Had I means of taking pleasure in wine
  I wouldn't wait for the fast to expire
Wine, when imbibed, is a marvellous thing
  So drink, even if the penalty's dire
Whoever would reproach the pure red draught
  Go to heaven, and leave me to the fire

As are:

Reproacher, obey me now
  And reduce your censure
And drink wine, and spare me
  From the daily prayer
If the time for praying
  Or fasting should occur
Banish the fast with drinking
  And swap prayer for slumber

And:

Someone asked: 'Would you do the Hajj?'[86] I said:
  Yes, were there no pleasure left in Baghdad

All quite brazen stuff; people were put to death for less in Europe not even two hundred years ago.[87] Yet to conclude on the strength of these lines alone that Abu Nuwas was a nonbeliever is, possibly, to miss the point. To see why, a quick digression on the poet's religious (or irreligious) views may be in order.

The first thing needing to be said at the outset – and too often overlooked – is that he wouldn't have been free to declare himself an apostate if he were one. For all the comparative liberties of the early 'Abbasid caliphate, it was still a theocracy, and heresy was a capital offence. Within Abu Nuwas' own lifetime, at least two prominent poets – Bashar ibn Burd and Salih ibn 'Abd al-Quddoos – were executed under the Caliph al-Mahdi on charges of heresy, and others, such as al-Hallaj, would go on to meet the same fate under later 'Abbasid caliphs after Abu Nuwas' death.[88] The poet plainly knew there were lines never to be crossed; even in poems where he boasts of committing sins, he is at pains to clarify these don't include polytheism (*shirk*),[89] which the Qur'an explicitly declares unpardonable.[90] It ought to go without saying, therefore, that wherever he does profess piety and devout religiosity – as in the *zuhdiyyat* – this must necessarily be treated to some extent as testimony made under duress.

By the same token, that he did in fact utter so many impious verses despite the obvious risks, and continued to do so even after being jailed for the offence – when it was, in other words, very clearly not in his interest to do so – arguably compels us to attach greater weight to them as evidence, so to speak. Beyond the sort of thing quoted above, moreover, are lines more incriminating still, such as the small number of extracts listed in the *Diwan* as 'infidel verse' (*kufriyyat*), containing ostensible repudiations of Judgment Day and even the afterlife altogether. Were this an Inquisition, the cardinals might well imagine their case at this point to be open-and-shut.

And yet it's still entirely possible to argue he was, in fact, a perfectly sincere Muslim. It isn't necessarily relevant here that he knew the Qur'an by heart since childhood, and had mastered the Hadith to the extent that he taught it to pupils including the seminal theologian al-Shafi'i and the celebrated essayist al-Jahith (to this day, at least two Hadiths bear Abu Nuwas' name in their chain of transmission).[91] Nor should we overstate the significance of his occasional declarations of repentance, which tended to be made when he was trying to get out of jail, and which even apologetic commentators concede were mostly disingenuous or fleeting.[92] (The poet himself begins one verse with: 'People say, "You've repented"/ No, by God, I haven't'.)[93] It isn't the times Abu Nuwas claims to forswear drink, but rather those when he endeavours to reconcile it with Islam that merit our real attention.

It is essential to keep in mind that Abu Nuwas lived at a time well before the crystallization and consolidation of Islamic doctrinal orthodoxy as we now know it. The creedal topography, indeed, of Islam in the poet's lifetime differed almost unrecognisably from today's. Many denominations now taken for granted as inseparably intrinsic and integral to Islam – Salafism, Wahhabism, Druzism, 'Alawism – were then still decades if not centuries from formation. If Sufism could have been said to exist at all it was embryonic at most, confined to a fringe sub-clique of ascetics then better known as *nussak* (sing. *nasik*); certainly the elaborate mystic doctrines expounded by the likes of al-Ghazali (d. 1111) and Ibn ʻArabi (d. 1240), the poems of Rumi (d. 1273) and Hafez (d. 1390), and the *turuq* institutions and whirling dervishes and other now-signature accoutrements of Sufism were several centuries in the future. Shiʻism of a kind had existed since the Prophet's death, though its prevailing form today, known as Twelverism, self-evidently wasn't known to Abu Nuwas, since the eponymous Twelfth Imam had not yet been born.[94] Similarly, while there was a proto-Sunni movement of a sort – in that there were clerics who stressed the primacy of Hadiths over other, speculative tools of theology – this was scarcely identifiable as the Sunnism of today, nor was it regarded as the mainstream or leading strain of the faith. To the contrary, its adherents were only one of over half a dozen contending factions (many now extinct) that had cropped up in the Rashidun and Umayyad eras, including the aforementioned Khawarij, and were if anything eclipsed by the philosophically-inclined Muʻtazila, whose assertion that the Qur'an was created (as against the proto-Sunni belief in its uncreatedness) would come to be enforced as official state dogma, on pain of execution, by the Caliph al-Ma'mun shortly after Abu Nuwas' death. (It was only indeed the eventual abolition of this dogma and its replacement with proto-Sunnism by the Caliph al-Mutawakkil in the mid-ninth century that opened the door for the ascendance of Sunni orthodoxy as we now think of it.)[95]

A third of these then-prominent, now-vanished factions were the Murji'a, whose core doctrine of *irja'* ('postponement') held that the question of whether one could sin and remain a Muslim ought to be put off till the afterlife, when God Himself would make His own judgment. To their opponents' contentions that those who committed grave sins (*kaba'ir*) were destined for hell, the Murji'a could retort with Qur'an 39:53: 'Verily, Allah forgives all sins' (with the aforementioned exception of polytheism). Indeed, divine forgiveness (*ghufran*), they said, was available to any Muslim, no matter how morally compromised, who believed faithfully in his heart. (It's perhaps not very surprising that in their English-language magazine, *Dabiq*, the Islamic State has denounced *irja'* as 'the most dangerous' of heresies, saying, 'Allah's mercy and forgiveness is [sic] not an excuse to commit sins and injustices never mind shirk [polytheism] and kufr [disbelief]!')[96]

Certainly, the emancipatory possibilities of the doctrine were not lost on Abu Nuwas, who, as well as making light of (proto-Sunni) Hadith literalists in general,[97] often espoused explicitly Murji'i tenets, even if he didn't name them as such. 'Drink wine, though it be prohibited/ For Allah grants forgiveness [*ghufran*] for grave sins [*kaba'ir*]', reads one line.[98] Another, more mischievous, verse begins: 'Commit as many sins as you can/ For you shall meet a forgiving Lord'[99] (the word used for 'forgiving', *ghafoor*, appears in the same Qur'an verse cited in the previous paragraph). Perhaps most famous is the closing line of his celebrated CEASE YOUR REPROACH, slapping down an illustrious Mu'tazilite theologian, Ibrahim al-Natham, who had rebuked the poet for his wine drinking: 'Don't forbid forgiveness if you choose to abstain/ For that forbiddance is, of faith, desecration.'[100] This is Abu Nuwas in the role of Murji'ite militant, asserting it isn't just ignorant or mistaken but actually blasphemous to deny the totality of God's forgiveness.

Needless to say, all this may very well have merely been an elaborate ruse on the poet's part; a silver bullet enabling him not only to keep up his lifestyle unimpeded, but to claim the God-given right to do so. In general, it pays ill to read any writer of the ironic with too literal a mind, and to picture Abu Nuwas seriously wrapped up in doctrinaire zealotry and sectarianism is all but impossible. In the end, whether or not Abu Nuwas really was a believing Muslim, he was careful to leave enough evidence that he *could* have been. Thus could he persist in having all things all ways, the joke forever being at the expense of anyone who took anything he said too seriously.

If the *khamriyyat* show Abu Nuwas to be a voice for what we might nowadays term liberalism or even secularism in religious matters, they also reveal a pronounced tendency toward a kind of cosmopolitan humanism in the political domain. For a start, there isn't a trace of any hostility in his many depictions of Christians, Jews, Zoroastrians, and other religious minorities (on the contrary, they are lauded for their approbation of wine). The same goes for the various non-Arab ethnic groups with whom the poet came into contact, from Kurds to Assyrians to – especially – Persians.

The latter, indeed, feature very prominently in the poems. On the face of it, this may seem unsurprising, given the eminence Persians enjoyed in 'Abbasid government and society, and the fact that Abu Nuwas' own mother was Persian. Yet to glorify Persian history and culture with the fervour that he did – to the extent of denigrating Arab heritage, portraying it as a trivial and savage sideshow to centuries of gleaming Persian civilisation – was to take no small political and personal risk. For one thing, it could (and did) invite accusations of closet Zoroastrianism or Manichaeism (*zandaqa*), a crime of heresy for which many had been executed from the Caliph al-Mahdi's era onward.[101] More broadly, relations between Arabs and Persians, though warmer than they'd been under the Umayyads, were still inevitably somewhat strained under the 'Abbasid rulers, who based their legitimacy on their membership of the (Arab) family of the Prophet, and were ever wary of the possibility of a major rebellion in (largely Persian) Khorasan, 'always the most recalcitrant province'.[102]

For Abu Nuwas, then, to write poems celebrating Nowruz, the Persian New Year (and holiest Zoroastrian festival), and to praise wine as the 'heritage of Anushirvan,[103] not that/ Left by Tameem or Bakr's brigade',[104] was to taunt officialdom in more ways than one. Yet it would be a mistake to think of him as any sort of Persian chauvinist. For all his mockery of the Arabs in certain verses, in others he boasts of his own membership (through his father) of the Yemeni al-Hakam clan, even partaking in the internecine feud between the northern and southern Arab tribal confederations. As Philip Kennedy writes, 'he doubtless considered himself overwhelmingly to be an Arab poet'.[105] Which isn't to say he wasn't also at ease with Persian and other components to his identity. Most educated Baghdadis of the time were in any case 'more or less bilingual in Persian and Arabic',[106] and Abu Nuwas could throw Persian as well as Syriac words and phrases into his lighter verse.[107] There are *khamriyyat* marking the festivities of Nowruz, Palm Sunday, and 'Eid al-Fitr. This is only contradictory if one insists on reading it humourlessly, and forgets that Abu Nuwas' concern was never petty factionalism or ethno-nationalist jingoism but rather the crafting of amusing and ingenious poems above all else.

In few verses is this plainer than his satires on warfare, which must surely rank among the oldest examples of anti-war poetry in world literature. Part mockery of the heroic posture of the old Arabic corpus (where convention dictated that poets boast of their martial prowess); part commentary on actual wars that took place in his lifetime; the message is – as ever – that we'd all be better off just drinking wine and going to bed with one another:

O Bishr,[108] what do I want with swords and war
When I was made for pleasure and delight?
Place no confidence in me, for I'm
Spineless in the heat of battle and fight
[…]
Were it but revelry, and drinking
With floral-necklaced[109] girls all night
And sleeping beside one to sup from
You would find me then the Arabs' knight

That particular poem pertains to a war against the Khawarij, possibly in Khorasan during Harun's latter years,[110] in which a friend (ludicrously) tried to persuade the poet to enlist. Others, with their mentions of catapults, mangonels, and similar heavy siege engines, appear to have the Amin–Ma'mun civil war in mind:

Our swords are roses and narcissi
Our insults are the words of the singer
Our mangonels are instruments
And 'ouds, once tuned and ordered
Our projectiles are filled wine cups
Fired off by their pourer

Our commander's a songstress
With lush jasmine we salute her
This is the war that we declare
Which harms not, but brings pleasure[111]

Pacifism; flowers; sex; drugs; and music: the poems might as easily have been written in 1960s Haight-Ashbury. If there ever, indeed, were any real guiding principle or creed to his politics, it was the bohemianism he'd first picked up in his teens, stumbling round the bars of Kufa with his mentor Waliba and the rest of the 'band of libertines' (*'usbat al-mujjan*). In a sense the *khamriyyat* are, in aggregate, almost a manifesto for this culture (or counterculture), in which wine is not merely an intoxicant but a muse; a lifeblood sustaining an entire intellectual, social, and moral worldview.

What else did this worldview comprise, beyond the aspects outlined above? And why was it wine, and not another drink, that was its sine qua non?

Well, on one level, of course, it *was* about intoxication – about feeling pleasure (*ladha*, or *tarab*) and driving off the everyday anxiety (*hamm*) of the human condition. A fine draught, in the poet's words, clothes its drinker 'in comfortable drapery'; brings out 'the wittiest joking'; and could 'inspire elation' even in cold stone. Equally, it 'repels worry' and 'assails woe'; in fact, 'Man has not found, nor experienced/ Anything like it to fight misery'.

In this, the poet anticipates the testimonies of countless other literary drinkers in later centuries. 'With wine I wash away my cares', said John Wilmot, the Earl of Rochester,[112] who is perhaps the closest thing to Abu Nuwas' English equivalent (with Charles II as his al-Amin). Kingsley Amis could have been paraphrasing the *khamriyyat* when he wrote, 'The human race has not devised any way of dissolving barriers, getting to know the other chap fast, breaking the ice, that is one-tenth as handy and efficient as letting you and the other chap, or chaps, cease to be totally sober at about the same rate in agreeable surroundings'.[113] From Johnson[114] to Housman[115] to Byron[116] to Burns,[117] the list of similar affirmations is lengthy.

Yet beyond the *carpe diem* and *ergo bibamus* elements, for Abu Nuwas wine also had other, loftier dimensions, pertaining to the sculpting of character and cultivation of ethics. Drink, for example, was prone to encourage the much-esteemed virtue of generosity (*karam*), even in a seasoned miser (*shaheeh*). It also engendered such qualities as sincerity, even-temperedness, forbearance, and good humour, as neatly summarised in the opening lines of SEIZE THE NIGHT'S REMNANTS, AND BE DRUNK:

A sincere drinks partner – nay, he adds humour
  To sincerity, and is never querulous
Carrying what I make him carry, unvexed
  Bearing what would irk the generous
He gave me, from the daughter of his soul,
  His whole love, and shared his riches[118]

In *The Wine Song*, Philip Kennedy shows how these and other traits associated by Abu Nuwas with drinking mirror the traditional Bedouin mores of *muruwwa* (literally 'manhood'; used in the sense of honour and chivalry, akin to Latin *virtus*), as contrasted with *jahl* (literally 'ignorance'; more broadly meaning foolish or improper conduct), of which he accuses non-drinkers.[119] (If there's an irony in this appeal to the same conventional value system he elsewhere ridiculed so thoroughly, it can only be at his antagonists' expense.) With this flourish, the poet completed his defence of wine, having thus made its case on grounds cultural and political; secular and religious; hedonistic and pious; modernist and, finally, traditionalist.

It might be wondered why the word 'Islamic' has been used next to the words 'wine poetry' in this book's sub-title. It's the hope of the author that, by the end of the book, the reader will be able to return the question: why not? Wine has, after all, ever been a permanent fixture of the Islamic universe. The social and cultural landscape into which Islam was born was steeped in drink, as the rich poetry of the unfortunately-named *Jahili* ('Ignorant') period amply attests. In the Qur'an, God Himself declares that wine has 'benefits for the people,'[120] and indeed its consumption was fully permissible (*halal*) during Islam's earliest years, when the Prophet was still in Mecca and for a time after his migration to Medina in 622. For the Prophet's Companions (*Sahaba*), to drink during this period was routine; in fact it was precisely because a group of them, led by the esteemed ʻAbd al-Rahman ibn ʻAwf, had got drunk at a lunch and then misrecited the Qur'an at the evening prayer that the verse came down forbidding drunkenness at prayer times, according to orthodox exegesis.[121] While the Qur'an later took a stricter line, urging Muslims to 'avoid' wine entirely,[122] debate continued for centuries among theologians as to whether this amounted to a full proscription (*tahreem*),[123] and, if so, whether it applied to all intoxicating beverages or solely the powerful *khamr* made from grapes.[124] The Hanafi school of jurisprudence, for example, permitted consumption of the weaker raisin or date fermentation, *nabeedh*, and there are Hadiths alleging the Prophet himself drank the same (though it's generally held that his was not sufficiently fermented to have been alcoholic).[125]

In any case, Muhammad's 'court poet', Hassan ibn Thabit (d. c. 659), was certainly an accomplished wine bard in his pre-Islamic days, and continued to include wine scenes in his verse after adopting the new faith.[126] While he's said to have given up actually drinking the stuff once the Qur'an discouraged it, the same cannot be claimed for another of the Prophet's literary Companions, Abu Mihjan al-Thaqafi, a prodigious toper who famously almost missed the Battle of al-Qadisiyya in 636 due to the Caliph ʻUmar's commander having imprisoned him for drunkenness at the time (he persuaded someone to let him out, and by all accounts fought bravely in the battle).[127] Both poets had discernible influences on Abu Nuwas and were indeed quoted by him in tribute.[128]

Thus, never fully purged from the Muslim populace during the Prophet's lifetime, wine would forever remain a feature of Islamic society thereafter. Most caliphs were drinkers, starting with the Umayyad Yazid ibn Muʿawiya (d. 683) – drinks partner of the great wine bard al-Akhtal[129] – and continuing with few exceptions throughout the medieval age into the modern (Ottoman) caliphate.[130] Some of these must be counted among history's great imbibers. The Umayyad Caliph al-Walid ibn Yazid (d. 744), for instance, who went 'swimming habitually in a pool of wine of which he would gulp enough to lower the surface appreciably',[131] once brought 'wine and singing girls' along on pilgrimage to Mecca in an (ultimately abortive) attempt to transform the Kaʿba 'into a party tent'.[132] The Ottoman Sultan Murad IV (d. 1640), killed by the bottle at just 27, 'would shoot arrows at passersby from a window of the Topkapi Palace, or run disguised into the streets and kill random individuals with a sword, by way of inebriated amusement'.[133] Muslim sovereigns beyond the Ottoman territories were no less spirited: in the four decades that the Timurid Sultan Husayn Mirza Bayqara (d. 1506) ruled from Herat, in today's Afghanistan, 'there was not a day when he did not drink wine', and the Mughal Emperor Jahangir

(d. 1627), whose affection for drink exceeded even his love of opium,[134] went so far as to have coins struck depicting him luxuriously contemplating a goblet.[135] As we have seen, at least one reigning 'Abbasid caliph, and possibly a second, drank personally (and vigorously) in the company of Abu Nuwas.

Nor were caliphs alone with poets in this indulgence, naturally. Revellers at the Commander of the Believers' court or the innumerable gatherings outside Baghdad's city walls could include almost any member of respectable society, from princes to viziers to scholars to physicians. Leading doctors, indeed, wrote treatises positively recommending wine for its copious salutary qualities. For these same men to go on to write well-regarded commentaries on the Qur'an or *shari'a* would by no means be atypical.[136]

So ingrained, then, was wine in the classical Islamic period that the question is less how to reconcile the two than how to conceive of 'classical Islam' without wine. And if the two had blended in general since the outset of Islam's arrival, in the poetry of Abu Nuwas they became particularly, indeed inseparably, fused. Almost every one of the thirteen thousand lines he penned betrays an Islamic signature in one way or another, as should be no surprise for a writer whose very first literary frame of reference in childhood was the Qur'an. Some of his forays into Scripture and theology have already been aired in the above extracts, and readers will encounter many more in the coming pages. As with so much else, Abu Nuwas took this to creative extremes: one sub-group of comic poems, which could be dubbed *Qur'aniyyat*, features entire lines lifted verbatim from the holy book and slotted seamlessly into the metre and rhyme scheme.[137] Perhaps even more pertinent than the overt textual references, however, are the subtler linguistic and stylistic nods and allusions, which will also be highlighted below to the best of this author's abilities. Suffice it in sum to say Abu Nuwas' work could no more exist without Islam than Dante's or Milton's could without Christianity.

Does this suffice to call the *khamriyyat* 'Islamic'? In his influential 1974 study, *The Venture of Islam: Conscience and History in a World Civilization*, Marshall G.S. Hodgson defined the adjective rather austerely as follows: 'When I speak of Islamic literature, I am referring only to more or less "religious" literature, not to secular wine-songs, just as when one speaks of Christian literature one does not refer to all the literature produced in Christendom.'[138] Granted, one probably does not refer to the 'Christian' novels of, say, P.G. Wodehouse, or Ian Fleming. One *might*, however, conceivably speak of the 'Catholic' comedies of Evelyn Waugh, and Graham Greene, and when faced with the likes of C.S. Lewis and G.K. Chesterton the 'Christian' label is practically inescapable. The obvious difference lies in the authors' treatment of the faith; how much Christian allegory or commentary or downright proselytisation is taking place; to what extent they are ultimately trying to say something intelligible and important about the religion. By this measure, the Islamicness of the *khamriyyat* can be in little doubt. The depth of the poems' theological involvement, as already sketched above, surely precludes their dismissal as exclusively 'secular wine-songs'. Much to the contrary, Abu Nuwas sought on some fundamental level in a great portion of his verse to make a fully serious statement about Islam – namely, that wine had a legitimate place therein. To deny the *khamriyyat* this label would be, in effect, to pronounce an Inquisitional verdict against the poet: to say that he was wrong about Islam and his prohibitionist opponents were right. Apart from anything else, it could hardly be the business of this non-Muslim author to handle so contentious a gavel.

Finally, just as the *khamriyyat* were inextricably bound up in the Islam of their time, so they and their author would leave their own imprint on later Islamic civilisation (or civilisations) in their turn. This is true even in the narrowly religious sense: that Abu Nuwas' name appears in the Hadith, which he taught to al-Shafi'i, has already been mentioned, and he makes further cameos in theological works as august as the Qur'anic exegesis (*tafseer*) of Ibn Kathir. In the wider cultural realm, his impact has naturally been weightier still. Beyond the *One Thousand and One Nights*, he features prominently in Arabic literary classics ranging from the *Kitab al-Aghani* ('Book of Songs') of Abu al-Faraj al-Isfahani (d. 967) to the *Murooj al-Dhahab*

('Meadows of Gold') of 'Ali al-Mas'udi (d. 956) to the *Risalat al-Ghufran* ('Epistle of Forgiveness') of Abu al-'Ala' al-Ma'arri (d. 1058). Stylistically, his 'extraordinary' influence is discernible everywhere from the mystic Sufi masterpieces[139] to the *muwashah* poetry of Andalusia to the novels of twentieth century North Africa;[140] Wagner goes as far as to say 'his works determined the entire range of later love poetry of the Arabs, the Persians, and the Turks'.[141] He has even become a figure of folk mythology in certain Muslim communities, about whom legendary stories are told in the vein of the Juha/Nasreddin character. In Zanzibar, for example, he's said by Ingrams to have been 'known as Kibunwasi, Bunwasi, Banawasi, or Abunwasi, more rarely, and by the "litterati" [sic] as Abunawasi'; a 'cunning' and benevolent champion of the underdog and everyman; 'quick of wit [...] a man who always has an answer ready, who excels in repartee – a man in fact who laughs best because he always laughs last'.[142]

None of which, of course, is to say he hasn't remained, as he was in his lifetime, out of favour with the sterner types within the Islamic establishment. This is, indeed, especially the case in our present era of puritan ascendancy. The story that thousands of copies of his *Diwan* were torched by the authorities in Cairo in 2001 appears on inspection to be untrue, though it was plausible enough to be believed by many.[143] What is not in doubt is that a statue of the poet on Baghdad's eponymous Abu Nuwas Street was vandalised in

July 2015 for, in the words of a local cleric, 'provok[ing] Muslims by manifesting drinking alcohol, which is forbidden in Islam'.[144] A monument honouring the preeminent poet of the 'Abbasid Golden Age, the clergyman went on, was 'not appropriate in a Muslim society'. (Happily, the Iraqi culture ministry disagreed, and restored the damaged marble).[145]

It certainly isn't hard to see what the Islamists find so threatening about him. While they would have Muslim society imagine an asphyxiatingly austere past as a model to be emulated today, Abu Nuwas' life and work testify instead to a 1,200-year-old tradition of liberty, satire, pluralism, and humour. While today's jihadists contend Islam is greatest when it is most dogmatic and despotic, the *khamriyyat* by contrast show the *umma* at its most successful precisely when the freedoms of thought, expression, and lifestyle are least repressed. To read Abu Nuwas is to be able to imagine an Iraq – indeed an entire Middle East – that is an utter and dazzling repudiation of the slaughter and hatred of today's news headlines. It's also to see that the secular and rationalist tendency, so often thought on both sides of the argument as something essentially Western, is in reality as Arabic, and Islamic, as Baghdad itself. It is, in other words, not so much to 'bridge' any 'gap' between the supposedly twain worlds as to enable one to see there need be no gap to speak of in the first place.

A Note on the Text and Translation

Abu Nuwas left no official compilation of his corpus (*diwan*). Versions of his poems can be found in several more or less contemporary works, most notably the ninth-century *Akhbar* ('Biographical Anecdotes') of Abu Hiffan, who knew the poet personally. Yet the first systematic attempts at collating his entire oeuvre were not carried out until the tenth century, by Abu Bakr al-Suli (d. 946), Hamza al-Isfahani (d. 971), and a third figure believed to have been Ibrahim ibn Ahmad al-Tabari Tuzun (d. 966). These anthologists strove to exclude apocryphal poems (of which many were in circulation), though al-Isfahani evidently had more relaxed selection criteria, for his recension is around three times the size of that of al-Suli,[1] who wrote of his contempt for 'ignorant' scholars 'who think that any and all poetry describing wine must be [Abu Nuwas']'.[2] The various manuscripts of these collections – some dating from as early as the eleventh century – scattered across libraries from London to Milan to Istanbul to Damascus[3] have been comprehensively amalgamated by Professors Ewald Wagner and Gregor Schoeler, whose resulting five-volume *Diwan* is the most authoritative in existence. It is on the fruits of Wagner and Schoeler's decades of backbreaking labour that these translations have been based.

However, even – or, rather, especially – within Wagner's *Diwan*, more than one variant of the same poem may exist (if, say, the al-Suli manuscript in Damascus differs by a word in one line from an al-Isfahani text in London). In most cases these discrepancies are trivial enough to make little or no difference in translation. In the minority of cases where they diverge substantively, I have tried to choose the word that seems the best fit in the context of the overall poem, or that is found in commercially available *diwans*, such as that of Dr. 'Ali Najeeb 'Atwi,[4] or that I simply happen to prefer. To determine with absolute certainty which text is the 'correct' one is of course not possible, and may be a fool's errand in any case: for all we know, Abu Nuwas might have recited different versions of the poems on different occasions.

Beyond that, to the extent I've adopted anything so grandiose as a translation methodology, it's been to maximise accuracy and fidelity to the original verses without, in Burton's words, 'offer[ing] up spirit at the shrine of letter'.[5] I have known the sheer fury, as a reader, of seeing a poem one loves in Arabic callously mutilated beyond recognition in English, and I've done everything in my power to avoid inspiring the same boiling rage in my own readers here. That I have opted to replicate the monorhyme structure of the originals has inevitably necessitated taking the occasional liberty with semantics – this, I firmly believe, is a price worth every penny to retain the rhymes without which so much of the poems' life expires. It's also one of the reasons I have only translated 125 of the slightly more than 300 *khamriyyat* in the *Diwan*; some run to over forty lines, which would entail finding as many words that all rhyme with one another; a pleasure I'm prepared to leave for another translator. (Plenty of shorter poems have also been omitted; some because I thought them similar to other, better ones; some because I'd never set out in any case to translate the corpus in its entirety. The selection in this book is intended instead as a distillation – I can only ask the reader to take my word for it that I never knowingly left out a poem that was both doable in rhyme and exceptionally interesting and/or amusing.)

The various Qur'an quotations in the foregoing and the following are largely my own renditions, crafted in consultation with the translations of Prof. M.A.S. Abdel Haleem (Oxford University Press, 2010), Prof. Arthur J. Arberry (Allen & Unwin, 1955), and the 'Saheeh International' text provided at quran.com and the related corpus.quran.com, among others, as well as the classical exegeses (e.g., of Ibn Kathir). All the usual *traduttore traditore* caveats about the imperfection of any non-Arabic Qur'an citation should of course be deemed fully operative here, as everywhere.

One cannot write a book that deals extensively in words and names of a foreign language without confronting questions of transliteration. There are, of course, formal academic conventions for Latinising Arabic, to which I've shown a measure of deference. On the one hand, I cannot bring myself, as some mavericks have, to write the Arabic letter *qaf* with a 'K' when the English alphabet provides us a perfectly serviceable 'Q'. For similar reasons I've been unable to resist inserting the established symbols denoting the pharyngeal fricative letter *'ayn* (') – except in the word 'Arab' itself, and its derivatives – and the glottal stop *hamza* ('): these are not mere accents but fully independent letters of the Arabic alphabet, and to omit them would feel like making a spelling mistake. On the other hand, I've tried to stay mindful of the dangers of fanaticism on this point. I'm not persuaded that 'al-Ḥaǧǧāǧ' (or indeed 'al-Ḥad̲jd̲jād̲j') is clearer for anyone than 'al-Hajjaj', and I'm no more inclined to write of 'Baššār ibn-Burd' than I would be to refer to Syria's 'Baššār al-Asad'. 'Bashar' seems fine to me, and, anyway, the only people to whom these hieroglyphics can be intelligible – that is, speakers of Arabic – will not require my assistance in pronouncing the words of a language they already know.

The poems' titles are my own creations; there being no Arabic convention for naming poems except, in well-known cases, by the last letter of each line (e.g., the '*hamziyya*' of Hassan ibn Thabit). Similarly, their order is arranged by themes of my choosing, rather than the Arabic norm of alphabetizing by the same final letter (which, needless to say, would be entirely arbitrary in English). Experts will notice

I've included several poems that, strictly speaking, fall outside the *khamriyyat* category as delimited in the Wagner-Schoeler *diwan* (which may classify them as panegyrics, for example, or lampoons). This, I would hope, is pardonable, given the multidimensionality even of poems clearly falling within one genre: the medieval recensors themselves often disagreed as to which verses belonged where. To this author, all poems that incorporate wine drinking, and even some that don't explicitly, are eligible for membership within the *khamriyyat*'s extended family.

I have made no attempt to reproduce the exact metres of the originals, which, per classical Arabic tradition, are uniform across all hemistichs; following one of as many as sixteen complex foot sequences. For this and all other injustices done to the poet's creations, I naturally take full responsibility, and can only hope he would be as forgiving to me as he wished Allah to be to him.

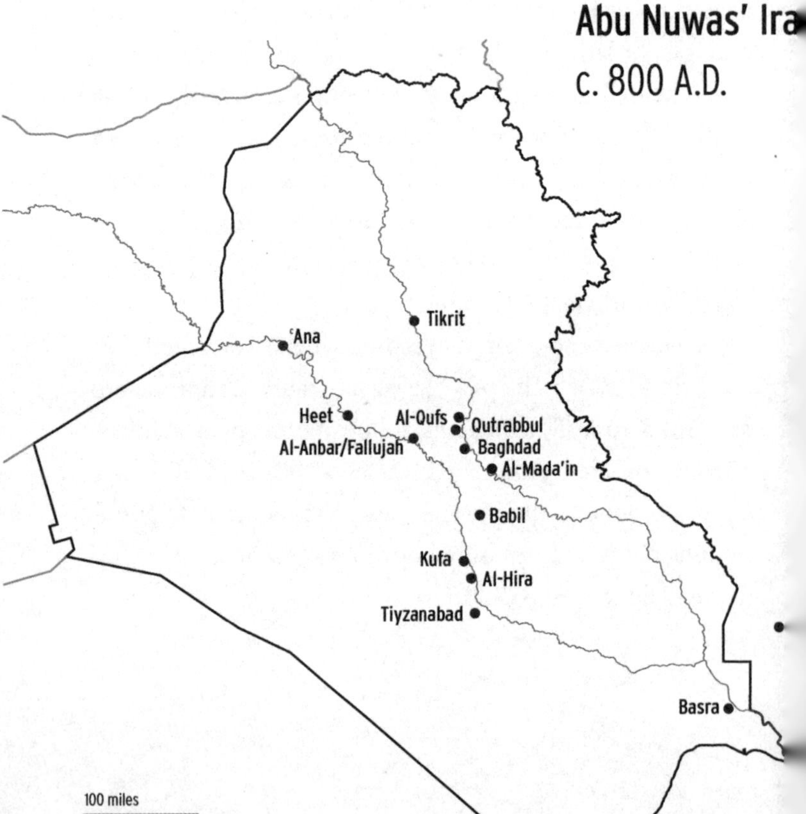
Abu Nuwas' Ira
c. 800 A.D.
Tikrit
'Ana
Heet
Al-Qufs
Qutrabbul
Al-Anbar/Fallujah
Baghdad
Al-Mada'in
Babil
Kufa
Al-Hira
Tiyzanabad
Basra
100 miles

Poems

I

‘What is Folly but Being Found Sober?’

Shorter poems of revelry

A Body without Soul[1]

I slowly, gently draw the spirit from the cask
        Seeking to sup from its bleeding hole
Till I'm filled with two souls in one body
        And the cask lies drained, body without soul

Wine and the Apple[2]

Wine is an apple in liquid state
        Just as an apple's wine in solid form
So drink the solid's liquid and don't
        Leave the pleasures of today for the morn

NB: According to al-Isfahani, 'He evokes in these two lines the saying of Aristotle: "The apple and wine are of one element, for wine is a liquid apple, and the apple is solid wine".'

We Turned, not to Fire, but Wine[3]

Many a freezing winter's day
When our faces, in snow, were mired
We turned, not to fire, but wine
That blazed within till we perspired

Expert Morning Drinkers[4]

Many a red wine yearner started early
With a group of expert morning drinkers
And all that he saw, he took for a glass
And each person he saw he thought a pourer

NB: Al-Isfahani writes that the poet al-Fadhl ibn 'Abd al-Samad al-Raqashi told Abu Nuwas he would trade everything he'd ever written to have composed these two lines. Some diwans, *but not Wagner's, include an extra line at the end: 'Till he sipped it, and in no time/ Was hurled to the floor, dead with no cure'.*

Pass It Around Us before We Part Ways[5]

Pass it around us before we part ways
Pour me the finest wine,[6] filtrated
For dawn's face will soon make the darkness smile
And the night's shawl will soon be lacerated

The Discharge of Pitchers[7]

Neither the racetrack nor the polo[8] field excites me
Nor do I long for the sparrow hawks' twitters
Life, instead, is in pleasures, reclined on pillows
And in song, and the discharge of pitchers

Is Our Wine Fire?[9]

Many a group of men has set out at dark
        Lightning flashing on hands and cups, entwined
A lamp was lit, and a pourer mixed the drinks
        And light filled the house like a lantern's shine
Startled, we asked him in confusion:
        'Is our wine the fire, or our fire the wine?'

The Vintner's Stock Grew Angry at You[10]

The vintner's stock grew angry at you
        When, in verse, you extolled her
She said: 'You compared me to fire
        'That dies when splashed with water
'While I'm one who – like dawn's star –
        'Gains beauty on mixture
'Thus I swear I'll deny you my milk
        'And make you drink the date-seller's'[11]

Babylon Wine[12]

Pass around sour Babylon wine[13]
Hand-selected from Caesar's aeon
Wine whose father's water, whose mother's the grove
Resembling a robe dyed saffron
What is folly but being found sober?
What's life but pleasure and inebriation?

Water's Wife[14]

Many a wine like clear agate
Fizzing with bright sparks, distressed
I've married with water to calm her
Yet she scorned the male caress[15]
Like a maiden on her wedding
Night, bashful to undress

The Pleasure of Life is Threefold[16]

The pleasure of life is threefold:
Wine, a comrade,[17] and a songstress
Drive off worry with aged wine, and know
That in wine the soul finds rest[18]
How often we've cured, with the glass,
Worries more bitter than death's stress

Wine and Temperament[19]

I see wine courses through the veins, and brings out
Concealed natures that spur disasters[20]
It increases the folly of the dim
But leaves noble souls undisturbed
I've found those least intelligent when drunk
Are the least so when sober

Pour Me Seven, Back to Back[21]

Pour me seven, back to back
        And pass them round with haste
Wine that, when poured, resembles
        How a light beam radiates
My dear friends, do drink up
        And lift the mask from your face
The sooner the critic starts
        The more he instigates

My Soul's Sister[22]

My critic in wine gives poor advice
        Spare my soul's sister[23] your calumny
Don't rebuke me for what enchants me
        And shows me the ugly un-ugly
Wine that renders the healthy ill
        And lends the ill the robe of the healthy[24]
My spending on her is generous
        And my possessiveness miserly

The Sheikh made Merry[25]

The sheikh made merry, and sang, and drank[26]
Of wine that strips joy of all sorrow
Drawing colour from each thing around it
Till its glass contains a rainbow
The sheikh of pleasures, pure in honour
For whom fine poetry's composed
You will not once find him without
Glass in hand as the wine jugs flow

Woe's Remedy[27]

Take pleasure in pale beauties
And in wine, and girls who sing
Be not dissuaded by critics
Who know, of your love, nothing
No remedy for woe exists
Like drinking from the morning
On my life, pure water
Is no cure for suffering

The Flute's Whimper[28]

If the church bell gave you joy
With the 'oud, and flute's whimper
And you began early with wine
Spat out by the grape clusters[29]
I took pleasure in a partner
They said, 'You're a rowdy waster'
Was there ever a rowdy man
Of sore heart, pained by love's rapture?

Death and Resurrection[30]

He befriended wine, thus time, for him, was short
And serene, without trouble or dismay
There are two states: death, and resurrection
For him who takes the cup every day
A glass of antique wine, whose scent,
Before the taste, leaves the mind disarrayed
Yellow-hued, its ribs red, its head
Shows the drinker the first signs of gray

The Hangover's Thrust[31]

How often a drinks partner poured for us
    While the morn was wrapped in the cloth of dusk
And he sipped till his night departed
    And dawn left him clothed in a robe, trussed
Then sleep overwhelmed him, and he jabbered
    For a while, until the hangover thrust
And he rose from his snooze, like a falcon
    And shook his head, whence came no dust

Drink not without Music[32]

Opt for a large glass, not a small
    Taken from a youthful beau
And spare me tears over courtyards
    And abodes lost long ago
Drink not without music, for horses'
    Thirst isn't quenched till the whinnies blow[33]
And drinking's not drinking without lutes
    Played on all strings high to low

Between Flute and String[34]

Movement of the eye and gaze
Is licit for the human being
My heart doesn't know restraint
And ill-endures suffering
I delight in the pourer, racing
Between flute[35] and string[36]
With wine whose body's with us
While its scent is travelling[37]

The Finest of Scents[38]

The scent of wine is the finest of scents
Bravo to all who guard it from stain!
Should you elect to drink it at a sitting
Keep your talk of men's flaws restrained
More important is the glass, and its thrills
So keep your discourse strictly on the twain
The smart fellow must select the sitters[39]
For the joy of gathering is repelling pain

Might You Perhaps Like the Nourishment of Wine?[40]

What compares to this day's splendour
	Put to fine use; joyous, carefree?
So what do you think? What is it
	You'd like to be today's activity?
Might you perhaps like the nourishment of wine
	That speeds through Man, if drunk quickly?
Man has not found, nor experienced
	Anything like it to fight misery

NB: Abu Hiffan (al-Mihzami, op. cit., pp. 39–40) narrates the following anecdote about this poem: 'Sulayman ibn Nawbakht told me: Abu Nuwas passed by me one morning in spring, and the sky had poured with rain for a while, and when he faced me at the door he started to recite [the poem].' Later, when night fell, and the pair had spent the entire day drinking, the visibly hammered poet said: 'My tongue divulges a hidden secret/ Namely, I'm a Time partisan/ There's no return after death/ Rather, death's egg is barren'. The reference to 'Time' (the line is more literally: 'That is, that I speak of Time') implies belief only in the earthly, material world, not in an afterlife – 'virtually a testament of* kufr *[disbelief]', as Kennedy says (*The Wine Song*, p. 135). According to Abu Hiffan's story, the poet then told his companion, 'Keep my secret, for drinking sessions are confidential'* (al-majalis bil-amanah; *literally, 'seated gatherings are confidential'; a profane play on this well-known saying attributed to the Prophet in the canonical Hadith collection of Abu Dawud, inter alia).*

** Ibn Manthur records an almost identical tale, but names Ahmad ibn al-'Abbas ibn al-Hakam instead of Sulayman ibn Nawbakht (op. cit., p. 130).*

What a Weapon Wine Is[41]

I see no pleasure, nor enjoyment
Nor success, till the glass is in sight
What a weapon wine is for man;
Assailing woe, and forcing its flight
Such wonders has wine that it could
Rid the miser of his spite
There's no life save that of drinking
From the morning till the night
Never shall I leave the glass, nor
Accept, in love, those who indict

Wine the Bride[42]

Pour me her, dear friend, in darkness
By the coal's light, not morning's blaze
Wine left in the cask by her vintner
For an age, untouched, locked away
Then married off in a black dress, adorned
Like a young bride on her wedding day
The gazelle fawn pours her in a glass
As she fires off sparkling rays
Her scent is of musk, so forceful
The drinker – smelling her – frowns, amazed

Wine and Woe[43]

Were the charms of the wine concealed from you
        Or were you changed by the caprice of Time?
For you have turned your face from the pearls
        And gold revealed by the smile of the wine[44]
Brought by a nasal-voiced coquet
        With eyes kohl'd as if with magic lines
And you forgot your saying, when you drank it
        And, like the stars of the Eagle,[45] declined:
'Do not suppose the wine of the cask
        'And woe can, in one chest, be combined'

Don't Cry for Layla nor Grieve for Hind[46]

Don't cry for Layla, nor grieve for Hind[47]
    Drink, instead, from rose-red wine
A cup which, once slid down the throat
    Grants the eye and cheek its crimson shine
For the wine is ruby, and the cup is pearl
    From the palm of a girl svelte and fine
Giving you wine from her hand, and her mouth
    So you can't but be drunk two times[48]
That's as I am, while the rest are drunk once
    Hers is a pleasure solely mine

NB: Both Harun and al-Ma'mun are said to have particularly enjoyed this poem. A marginal note in the Köprülü Library (Istanbul) manuscript of al-Suli's recension says Harun was once drinking with the Basran scholar al-Asma'i (d. 828) when the caliph asked the latter to recite 'the most enthralling' verse he knew on wine. When he delivered the above lines, the caliph asked whose they were. 'This young lad, al-Hasan ibn Hani", replied al-Asma'i. 'Don't belittle him, for he's the best of the modernists', retorted Harun, and ordered that Abu Nuwas be given twenty thousand dirhams.[49]

As for al-Ma'mun, al-Isfahani attributes to the musician Ishaq al-Mawsili a story that the caliph asked his guards if any of them could recite any poetry of Abu Nuwas'. When one came out with this verse, al-Ma'mun responded, 'That, by God, is poetry'.

Wine from Noah's Ark[50]

Get an early morning start
    And refuse, for wine, disdain
And pour me a draught that was
    Aboard Noah's Ark contained[51]
Wine that adds to you a soul
    So within you it leaves twain
With a scent you'd fancy perfume
    If a waft you did obtain
No one rides its boat, except
    That they find it unrestrained

II

'Have an Early Drink, and Enjoy Yourself'

Longer poems of revelry

Praise the Blessings of This Wine[1]

Praise the blessings[2] of this wine
        Grant it the finest epithet
Let not the water oppress it, nor
        Render it the water's despot
Wine of Karkh,[3] aged for an aeon
        Till most of it dissipated
And the vintner could not yield
        From it but its final spirit
It was passed round, reviving
        The souls of the discomfited[4]
A whole group of men could drink
        This wine, and yet never match it

Make Your Way to al-Karkh[5]

Make your way to al-Karkh
To a vintner's winery
To red wine, whose scent is like
The musk of a perfumery
To a field with palm trees
And flowers and shrubbery
There you shall be served the meat
Of birds and beastly quarry
Should you wish for entertainment
There's the piper's melody
And should you desire sex
Then have the landlady

NB: According to al-Isfahani, this poem was delivered in a live exchange with other poets, in which they competed to improvise short, amusing (and generally lewd) verses using the same simple metre – a genre known as naqa'idh; *literally 'contrasts'. The poets in question on this occasion were 'Ali ibn al-Khaleel al-Kufi, 'Amr al-Warraq, Dawud ibn Razeen al-Wasiti, al-Fadhl al-Raqashi, al-Husayn al-Khalee', al-Husayn al-Khayyat, Ibn Khazzaz, Isma'il al-Qarateesi, Razeen al-Kalbi, and a slave-girl called 'Inan. They were gathered on the banks of Baghdad's Sarat canal* (cf. HEAD TO THE SARAT'S BANKS) *one afternoon when the question was raised as to where they should spend the evening. Abu Nuwas suggested they each come up with a verse arguing for their preferred venue, and the above was his composition.*

Say to Whomever Weeps for a Vanished Abode[6]

Say to whomever weeps for a vanished abode
Standing, it wouldn't harm them to sit
You describe the place and Lubayna, and
Salma and Khanas who camped at it[7]
Put aside the dwelling and Salma, and drink
A morning glass of Karkh wine, firelit
Daughter of an age, kept in her cask
Distilled of all impure and unfit
Red as blood, so strong when tasted
Drinkers wince, with foreheads knit
Should you imbibe it with companions
Do so before dawn's rays have hit
And leave the ocean to seafarers[8]
Who are shameful and wretched

Head to the Sarat's Banks[9]

Abandon the old traces,[10] and give up
    Descriptions of homes and fire-poking
Leave the wretched Arabs to a
    Hopeless loser,[11] long-suffering
Head to the Sarat's[12] banks, and hand me –
    Pre-drawn, defying fools gibbering[13] –
A draught yellow as purest gold
    Fizzing with pearl bubbles, scattering
For I drink the vine's daughter, with funds
    New and old,[14] despite those envying
Karkh wine, clear as a lover's face
    White, too fine for kohl blacking
With a secret longing, so that between
    Her eyelids, tears start glistening
Afraid to shed them, she lifts her eye
    The tears between climbing and falling

What is Life?[15]

Free your morning of censorious speech
What is life except wine, crisp and cool?
What is life but that you start drinking, early
Yellow wine, married off from Qutrabbul?[16]
Wine that gifts pride to abased hearts
And tames the heart of the haughty and cruel
As though the delight of its scent brings
Its drinker's lips a floral bundle
I went to unveiled, full-breasted women[17]
Who greeted me with smiles, cheerful
I gained, from their witty discourse,[18] delight
As they did from me, and I was no fool[19]

Defy Those, Ignorant of Love, who Berate[20]

Have an early drink, and enjoy yourself
        And defy those, ignorant of love, who berate
Loosen the reins;[21] befriend every pleasure-seeker
        And join them wherever they congregate
Revelry, and the easy life, and finer
        Things are won by the witty reprobate
Pouring for young men, I drink with them
        Theirs is leather that won't lacerate[22]
This is for that one, just as this and this are for that one
        Thus do they bind their rope, and consolidate[23]
Honour them, and the tune of a songstress
        For in song proverbs initiate
A slender woman and an 'oud serenade us:
        'Bid Huraira farewell, the caravan awaits'[24]

Unmarried Wine[25]

Dispense, my friend, with all thought
        Of those who changed, or moved station
And drink sour wine, unmarried[26]
        Aged to incapacitation
From the palm of a soft deer
        Black-and-white eyed,[27] with flirtation
Stealing hearts with coquetry
        And, should he glance, with observation
It's as though within his palms
        Were the sun's and moon's illumination
The drinks partner hadn't finished
        Three before inebriation
With delight, he sang aloud
        Eyes no more in operation:
'You who sleeplessness torments
        'I have, of love, information'

There's No Surgeon Like the Glass[28]

I'll sever worry's aorta with the glass
For there's no surgeon like the glass for worry
Pour me fresh, crisp wine, stowed away
In her cask in a cellar's corner, buried
Yellow, with eyes like halves of bells
Leaving those poured smiling in glee
As though our glasses blazed in dark night
Like lamps in a deacon's apse, fiery
Enter a group of well-bred, cultured youths
Highborn; noble; not hoi polloi
I brought them yellow, crystal-clear wine
From a gazelle,[29] slim as a twig, haughty
His speech epicene, his eye seizing me
His face of Quraysh; 'Abbasi[30]
As though his chaplet were Ibn Mariya's[31] crown
When adorned with rose and myrtle posy
He may sing for you, when drunk and merry
As the glass struts to the sipper, proudly:
'By God, your splendour has scorched and tortured me
'From near and far, in hope and despondency'

Clouds of Woe[32]

Be not distracted from the grove's daughter
	For she pulls together the body's power
Know, if you intend on other than her,
	Clouds of woe shall rain upon you in showers
And if you see her foe at a gathering
	Approach him with ugliest rancour
And if you drink her, then savour her
	Till you reap the marvel of her flavour
And your uvulae enjoy her fineness
	As do the nostrils sniffing the odour
And look, if she faces you, in awe
	As an orphan would to the hand of the mother[33]
Did you not see the glass when you mixed her
	And she grew stupid, like a dullard?
Were there no comfort in drinking her
	There'd still be release from the hand of bother

Keep Her from the Water[34]

Have you bled her forehead with pure, clear water
        To hear her inside the glass, wailing?[35]
Your ears heard groans during the mixture
        And gabble replying to lamenting
Keep her, then, from water, and hand me her
        For if you don't, without her, I'm dying
In vessels carved of peridot, chosen
        By Khosrow[36] for their preserving
As though men of India surround her cup
        Perched on horseback, sides whirling[37]
By fingertips which the glass almost cuts[38]
        If its calm is spoiled by moving

Don't Mix Wine in Any Circumstance[39]

Don't mix wine in any circumstance
And pour the daughter of seasons
Aged by a Kurd at a drinks venue
Amongst gardens in the mountains[40]
He came to us, bowing his head
Down from the remote highlands
Holding a stoppered jug in his hand
Filled with blood-red potation
We took it from the palm of a soft-
Spoken boy, like a sculpture creation
He pours you wine with his eyes, when he
Whispers, with the glass, instigation
In no need of a kohl stick
Nor bracelet nor ankle decoration
A beauty spot adorns his cheek
What fine ornamentation!

Wine Like Ripest Rose[41]

Many a wine like ripest rose was
        Cleared by time of all flaws, unblended
Our pitcher is like a hilltop gazelle
        With neck, fearing the hunter, extended
A black-eyed one pours for you, expert
        In water-mixing, undergarmented
The full moon is no finer than him
        Praise God! He matched it when He created[42]
Nothing at all, when you see him, tops him
        As though he were, from heaven's garden, lifted
He kept mixing it once, then drinking it
        Once, till drunkenness cemented
Then he sang, as he turned his head round
        So his speech was ill-comprehended:
'The friend has departed once again
        'And the heart is, on Asma', suspended'[43]

Death by Drunkenness[44]

I purchased sin at a profitable price
        And sold piety for fine revelry
And made of debauchery my leash
        And found from it no remedy
And many a soft, henna-fingered lad;
        Flirtatious; face most comely
Did I conquer as dawn's star appeared
        He a Jesus devotee
He enjoyed my looks when he saw me
        Ascertained I wasn't miserly
So he took a spigot, and penetrated
        An old virgin, beyond flattery
She'd seen Noah when already grey[45]
        And lived, before Noah, for centuries
I poured for him till he died of drunkenness
        Though in no grave was he buried[46]

A Jewish Girl[47]

Drinks under a winemaker's roof
Rid me of all feelings dour
Especially with a Jewish girl, with
Eyes like moon at midnight hour
Pouring wine from her palm
Succulent as palm tree's flower
Once the drink courses through her
She obtains tremendous power
We turned toward her delights
As, to the Kharijite,[48] turn soldiers
So come with us, with a spigot
And dinar[49] if you seek pleasure
We have both, so don't be sluggish
And leave critics in the fire

A Hangover Piled on a Drinks Partner[50]

A hangover piled on a drinks partner[51]
        Causing his fingertips to jitter
He couldn't lift up his glass without
        His right hand beneath the left to bolster
I gave him a midnight cup of
        Frothy brew, and he got better
He said, 'Might you hand me a second
        'To calm me? I'd take another measure'
I said: 'Of course! And many more
        'I'll make them like horseback racers'
Such is our night habit, he and I;
        I pour, then he requests another
Till he collapses, unsure if it's
        On pillow or bare ground he slumbers

How Fine a Month is April![52]

The church bell called to you at dawn
        And the monk in 'Umr[53] began to sing
And the inebriate longed for wine
        And the rain answered by falling
Your eyes were taken by a meadow
        Greens and yellows appearing[54]
So give your companion wine
        Mixed from the stream by ladling
Among lavenders and buttercups
        And an androgyne in florid clothing
In a pasture, upon whose fringes
        White gazelle fawns are grazing
How fine a month is April!
        How fine, in 'Umr, is morn-drinking!
You, with *zunnar*[55] tied on the waist
        In the sanctity of the *fuhr*[56] or inn
Do not pour me, if you know me
        Except what my chest's concealing
Give me that which you know I love
        And allude to the wine by anything[57]
Enough of my doubting[58] your mixing[59]
        Which may covet betraying[60]
How fine is openness in youthful passion
        When you aren't, from your Lord, hiding

NB: Al-Isfahani writes that a drinking companion of Abu Nuwas' named al-Muthaffar ibn Hayyan told of being in al-Hira (see I MISS AL-HIRA; O HANNA MONASTERY*) with the poet on a rainy night when 'drunkenness overcame me, and I slept, and Abu Nuwas stayed sitting and drinking, and [later] woke me, saying, "Damn you, do you not see this rain? Do you not smell this breeze? Do you not hear the sound of the church bell?"' and then he recited the above poem.*

Your Reproach Comes from Envy[61]

The wretch stopped to question the trace,[62] and I
Stopped to ask for the vintner of the country
He weeps for those gone from the Asads[63]
Damn you, tell me: Who are Asad's progeny?
And who are Tameem, and Qays, and their brothers?[64]
North Arabs, to God, are nobodies[65]
May God not dry eyes weeping for stones
Nor grant those pining for tent pegs relief
How different's one who buys and enjoys wine
From one who rocks and stars cause to weep
Forget them, and drink an aged wine
Yellow, spread between soul and body
From the palm of a slim one, with short *zunnar*
Straight as a ben[66] branch, not droopy
Don't you see the land's faces in bloom;
Clothed by the Lion's Nose[67] in tapestries?
Spring has embroidered the soil, and covered it
In ripe, singled and doubled greenery
And the wine has finished its years of ageing
And your life has revealed new glee
So drink and be generous with your holdings[68]
Don't hoard today fearing tomorrow's poverty

O critic, in your anger you insult me
    If I forgive you, don't be angry
If your reproach were advice, I'd take it
    Yet your reproach comes from envy[69]

I Gained What He'd Withheld[70]

Keep me from people, and their reproach
And sip the grove's female offspring
And weep for what's gone from her, and don't
Weep for an old Awtas dwelling[71]
For wine shall benefit you twice:
When bankrupt, and when prospering
Basil poured from a palm of basil
By myrtle and carnation, blossoming
A young, nasal-voiced one greeted us
Able to silence, or prompt speaking
He was about to grant me his lips' taste
If not for the people watching
How many a night I've spent in pleasure
With a gazelle fawn, white, strutting
And we partook of red Karkh wine
Poured out with precise measuring
And I drank from his lips once
Then once again from the glass' settlings
And when the drink had worn out his speech
What spoke instead were Satan's musings
And I managed to unbind his trousers
After I'd given up hoping

Till he fell over, like one love-crazed
        And sleep embraced the others sitting
And I gained what he'd withheld when sober
        As my heart raced with wildest pounding
There's never any fun in pleasure, unless
        Its participants' heads are showing[72]

III

'Pour Me the *Haram* before the *Halal*'

Poems (un)concerned with piety

The Wine in Heaven[1]

As for that which is forbidden
Whatever could be dafter?
A thing banned in this world
Yet abounds in the hereafter[2]

The Wine Bargain[3]

This is the wine of which it is
Said to us: 'Don't drink it
'Avoid it, O sons of pleasure
'That we fill your goblet[4]
'Lend us a glass in a pouch
'Tomorrow we'll repay it'
Thus if I arrive at it, I'll
Fast till you remove it[5]

The Polytheists are Protection[6]

Screw all the fine ones you find
And drink the banned refreshment
For the polytheists are protection
For the Muslims from torment[7]

Your World's a Fleeting Dwelling[8]

Leave the traces,[9] give them no thought
Truly, but woe, they bring nothing
And drink wine, though it's forbidden
For your world's a fleeting dwelling
Wine that, he who sees it, says:
'Our cups caught the sun while hunting'

I Wept for the Wine[10]

I wept, and not for old traces[11] passed by
Nor have I a lover to bring tears to the eye
Instead, a Hadith came from our Prophet
Spurring sobs till my chest wasn't dry[12]
Decreeing drink a sin, forbidding it
And when it forbade it, for the wine did I cry
Still, I drink it, straight, knowing well that
To my back, eighty shall be supplied[13]

Luqman's Wisdom[14]

I took an oath to drink fragrant
Wine of Falluj and 'Anat[15]
Wine of a kind like no other
Swearing by 'Uzza and by Lat[16]
If Luqman, with all his wisdom[17]
Drank five glasses from its vat
He'd bow down, pitcher in hand, to
Insolent heresy on his prayer mat[18]

Don't Depart from al-Qufs[19]

O 'Amer, don't depart from al-Qufs[20]
        Let's drink wine, yellow as saffron
We'll steal this day from our month
        For God may give thieves pardon

*NB: Al-Isfahani writes that the 'day' referred to here is the so-called Day of Uncertainty (*Yawm al-Shakk*), which can either be the first day of the lunar month of fasting, Ramadan, or the final day of the preceding month, Sha'ban, depending – per Islamic custom – on whether the new moon is sighted during it. According to al-Isfahani, one year Abu Nuwas and a friend named 'Amer spent the month of Rajab (preceding Sha'ban) in the village of Qutrabbul, moving thereafter to al-Qufs for the duration of Sha'ban. When the Day of Uncertainty arrived, 'Amer wanted to depart for Baghdad in case it turned out to be the first of Ramadan, but the poet persuaded him to stay and drink away one last day; thus 'stealing' it from the month of fasting. (Ibn Manthur records a slight variation of the same story, in which the poet's companion is a member of the Nawbakht family [op. cit., p. 127].)*

Go to Heaven[21]

Had I means of taking pleasure in wine
        I wouldn't wait for the fast to expire
Wine, when imbibed, is a marvellous thing
        So drink, even if the penalty's dire
Whoever would reproach the pure red draught
        Go to heaven, and leave me to the fire

NB: Both Abu Hiffan and al-Isfahani write that Abu Nuwas was with a Muhammad ibn Zuhayr during the month of Ramadan when the latter asked the poet how he was coping without wine during the daytime. Not very well at all, was the gist of his reply, which was followed by his reciting the above poem. Muhammad ibn Zuhayr is also mentioned in connection with THE PLEASURES OF BAGHDAD.

Banish the Fast with Drinking[22]

Reproacher, obey me now
    And reduce your censure
And drink wine, and spare me
    From the daily prayer
If the time for praying
    Or fasting should occur
Banish the fast with drinking
    And swap prayer for slumber
All your life, oppose the habits
    Of one people after another

We have Tired of You[23]

How much longer are you staying, O month?[24]
We've sickened and tired of you
Were one able to kill months
We'd have crucified[25] you
In the same way we have praised
Shawwal,[26] we've derided you
How we yearn for the day
We need no more abide you

The Wittiest Joking[27]

The fast departed, and Fitr came with joy[28]
And the glass brought out the wittiest joking
And pleasure visited you in its turn
Renewed between the cup and ʿoud string
Nothing was heard but the singer's voice
Fatigued by night-long requesting
And the wine stood out in finest robes
And all were drunk, or drinking till morning

Take Revenge on Ramadan[29]

Take revenge on Ramadan
With the fine wines aged in clay
And spend Shawwal in revelry
As the songstress plays
May you be, without exception
Drunk at least twice a day
Shawwal has been most generous
Our thanks must be conveyed
It brought festivity and song
And kept the fast's shackles at bay
The months I find most agreeable
Are, from Ramadan, furthest away

Ramadan's Fast Forbade Us Wine[30]

Ramadan's fast forbade us wine
And drained of us all joy and glee
We remained locked in its cells
Prisoners of misery
Now, however, we'll be kind
To those who weren't treated kindly[31]
We shall drink from dusk till dawn
From cups both tall and tiny
If one of our men has gone
We'll drink to his memory
And we'll sing without restraint
What we desire of poetry
Pour me drinks until you see me
Take the rooster for a donkey[32]

The Pleasures of Baghdad[33]

Someone[34] asked: 'Would you do the Hajj?'[35] I said:
Yes, were there no pleasure left in Baghdad
Or Qutrabbul, from where I spy
The dome of Firk at the fringe of Kalwad
Or Salihiyya, or Karkh[36] that gathered
The finest deviants of Baghdad
Why would I go on Hajj as long as
I'm plunged in a wine house, or pimp's pad?
And even could you save me from those
How could I be saved from Tiyzanabad?[37]

'Will You Turn Pious after the Hajj?'[38]

They asked: 'Will you turn pious after the Hajj?' I said:
        I hope in the Lord, and fear Tiyzanabad[39]
I'm afraid, even if I hurry, the smallest
        Twig of its orchard may hold my camel back
What drives piety from a heart, and splits it
        Are Qutrabbul, and Qura Binna, and Kalwad[40]
And if I evade them – hardly a certainty –
        I surely can't do the same in Baghdad
A place with all the gardens you could want
        Alas, therein are tribes and clans
A people whose tradition's forsaking holiness
        You say 'This is evil', and, 'That's bad'
Not like those who, if you see them in session
        You're speared with lances of reprimand
There no reproach transgresses your ear
        Nor does anyone say 'What?' or 'Who's that?'

Hand Me a Glass to Distract[41]

Sing for me, O Sulayman[42]
        And, of wine, do pour me
Should the bottle come your way
        Seize it, and pass hastily
Do you not see morning's sun
        Appearing in its drapery?
Hand me a glass to distract
        From the muezzin's melody[43]
Pour me wine without disguise
        And take me in sodomy

Aim for the Noble Sins[44]

Rid yourself of what makes them solemn
        And, should you pass a den of vice, enter
Do not commit, of sins, the vile ones
        Aim, if tempted, for the nobler
A sin that costs its buyer dearly
        Never losing its flavour
Not the kind of which the lad says
        In remorse: 'Would that I'd demurred'
I've freely turned the *haram* to *halal*[45]
        And, maybe, indulged what I should have abjured

NB: Al-Isfahani writes of a story told by Sulayman ibn Abi Sahl ibn Nawbakht in connection with this poem. Abu Nuwas, said Sulayman, got drunk one evening after the breaking of the fast (iftar) *during the month of Ramadan, and ended up sleeping with a man. When Sulayman reproached the poet for this, the latter responded in writing with the above verse.*

I Drink Wine[46]

When they brought me a glass of their beverage
Called *tila'*; some strong draught they'd acquired[47]
I proclaimed piously: 'I drink wine
'God Himself knows wine's my desire'
Their chief swore that by fire was it cooked
As though he praised it with such mire
I said, 'Whoever tortures wine with flame
'May God not ease his pain in the fire'[48]

*As Sidqi notes (*Alhan al-Han*, pp. 202–7), the practice of cooking wine was relatively widespread in the poet's time, as it was deemed by some religious scholars to render the drink's consumption permissible (*halal*). Whether due to its taste, or simply on principle, Abu Nuwas harboured what Sidqi calls an 'intense hatred' of these cooked wines, including the *tila'* *mentioned here (cf.* O, DAUGHTER OF THE SHEIKH, POUR FOR US*). It's no accident that when he says above, 'I drink wine', he specifically uses the word* khamr, *which not only denotes conventional, uncooked wine, but was the term for the one intoxicant practically all Muslim theologians agreed was forbidden (*haram*). The poem is thus a fairly brazen repudiation of the clerical establishment, as well as another example of the poet half-seriously suggesting it is in fact abstainers from* khamr, *not its consumers, who constitute the real sinners (c.f.* CEASE YOUR REPROACH; WE HAVE, IN THIS LIFE, HEAVEN'S WINE; DEFY THOSE, IGNORANT OF LOVE, WHO BERATE*).*

Wine's Brother[49]

I left *tila'*; I don't go near it
Why would I give my enemies delight?
Its brother, however, from aged raisins[50]
Can, if drunk sufficiently, excite
Wine's brother, from the same grape bunch
Except that it's been dried a few nights

NB: The poet ordinarily disdained nabeedh *(see second note) almost as much as he did* tila' *(see* I DRINK WINE*). An anecdote told by the grammarian and critic al-Mubarrad (d. 898), quoted by al-Isfahani, purports to explain the poet's ostensible change in tone here. The story goes that one day the Caliph al-Amin found Abu Nuwas intoxicated, despite the former having expressly forbidden him from drinking (cf.* I DON'T TASTE THE WINE EXCEPT BY NOSE*). 'Did you not proclaim repentance?' the caliph asked him. 'Yes, from drinking* khamr, *and I, like everyone else, have not drunk* khamr *[now]' replied the poet, and recited the above verse.*

Al-Amin then went with him to the venue at which he'd been drinking, where in fact the aroma of khamr *was unmistakable. Thinking on his feet, the poet spontaneously quoted Qur'an 12:94: 'I detect the smell of Joseph, if you do not think me weakened in mind', at which the caliph laughed, and said, 'Drink it, for there's no weakness in your mind'.*

Pour Me the *Haram* before the *Halal*[51]

Pour me the *haram* before the *halal*[52]
    And spare me vanished remains of campsites[53]
For life is in early wine drinking
    And inebriety dawn till night
Consummate joy lies in a pourer
    Of fine visage, beauty shining bright
Were his face to appear at sunrise
    You'd say the two were of the same light
So pour me wine, fine as a garment
    That rids me of camels, kneeling in respite[54]

Rebuke Brings Me Naught[55]

You who criticises wine
Since when were you so dim?[56]
You were just the same as me
Until this pious whim
Between your and God's reproach
I'd sooner yield to Him
So, my friend, have a glass of
Morning wine, and fill my brim
For rebuke brings me naught, save
Desire for the beaker's rim

Let Wine Repel Misery[57]

Morning's radiance has shone
        So let wine repel misery
Shame on those who would shun
        The drinks partners for piety
Tell him who covets holiness
        I sold mine for depravity
The sensible hand triumphed
        And sold, for sin, fidelity
The best of pleasures are those
        Exposed to full publicity

What are People[58]

Dawn has torn apart the veils of darkness
        Gone is the black night was clothed in
So pour your friends a sooty draught that
        Spent, in the cask, a duration
Daughter of an arbour, pleasant to drink
        Watered by autumn's season[59]
Married off to her noblest suitor
        Rose and jonquil are her linen[60]
One with black-and-white eyes[61] brings her
        Wearing an enchanting grin
What are people but a libertine rake
        Or a man sobered by religion?

Given God's a Pardoner[62]

Forgo temperance in drinking
        And take a glass, with vigour
Of wine like the dazzle of
        Lightning in its tumbler
And link up with every beau in
        Cotton robes, with waist slender
Why – tomorrow on hell's bridge[63]
        Given God's a pardoner
– would forgiveness be created
        But for those who err?

Give Back My Glass[64]

Give back my glass, for you two
Do not grasp its utility
You've tried to make me fear God but
My fear's offset by His mercy[65]
Rebuke not the wine, for you know
Not what it brings devotees
If it gave you what it gives me, you'd
Mix it with tears of ecstasy
Show me anything equal to wine
In fineness and amity
But for the touch of lips on a cheek
Nothing's like its felicity
Should you abstain, fearing God's wrath
So be it – I'll drink without company

NB: Al-Isfahani comments: 'He was drinking khamr *with a group of* nabeedh *drinkers, who encouraged him to drink* nabeedh *instead, telling him to fear God for drinking* khamr, *so he recited [this poem]'. As discussed in the introduction, a distinction was made at the time between these two drinks;* nabeedh *being a weaker one permitted by some theologians, while the stronger* khamr *was almost universally proscribed. Today* nabeedh *is a standard word for wine of all kinds. See also* *DISREGARD HIM WHO REBUKES IT; A CLERIC'S FATWA.*

The Drink and the Qur'an[66]

Pour for me, and pour for Yusuf
        Wine that provokes jitters[67]
Keep from life everything that
        Is clouded, and take what's clear
Pour me it completely full
        I desire no half-way measure[68]
Place the drinking pouch aside
        And set a Qur'an down near
And sip, from that, three times
        And recite, from that, letters
Virtue here, and evil there
        Thus is life uncluttered
Sin and then repentance
        For, if God's a forgiver,
The winner is he who cancels
        That with that, and finds pleasure[69]

If I Sought Probity[70]

They said 'You've abstained', not knowing my wish
For every delicate, cool-faced, young strutter
How could I abstain, when my heart's been torn
By the glance of eyes, and the wine's colour?
If I sought probity, I'd be fenced in
By two opinions;[71] on my ease, and lucre
For ease lies in days of free-spending revelry
And hardship lies in coupling with my lover[72]
Life is no good without aged wine
And its equals; rose, myrtle, gillyflower
And a singer to serenade, and glasses
Thrust upon us, five and six in number:
'You, with the fire iron whose tenders have tired
'Kindle, if you like, from my heart with your poker'[73]

How to Abstain?[74]

How to abstain from youthful passion and the glass?
Riddle that, critic, with something to compare[75]
Adding up my years, I find no excuse
For the greyness that sprouts in my hair
They said, 'You've greyed'; I said, 'Well my hand
'In thrusting the glass to my mouth's not impaired'[76]
Yellow draught, its comeliness adorned
Given, by its sipper's praise, new flair
So radiant, it's as though its drinker
At night, sups by coal ember's glare
More pleasant than the gifts of a lover's company
Acquired after hardship and despair
Wine is excellent, yet incomplete
Without the excellence of those in the chairs[77]
If you must abstain from sin, then let
That be for God, not a human affair

NB: Certain diwans, *though not Wagner's, include an extra line at the end here: 'And should you wish to praise a people, without lying/ Let it be, for the sons of 'Abbas, declared'.*

We have, in This Life, Heaven's Wine[78]

Someone came to reproach me with an innovation[79]
    A plan of which I can bear zero toleration
Urging me off wine, because the fate of
    He who tastes it's eternal damnation
These rebukers bring me nothing but resolve
    To grant wine my lifelong dedication
Shall I spurn it, when God Himself hasn't[80]
    And our own caliph shows it veneration?
Superlative wine, radiant and bright
    Rivalling the very sun's scintillation
While we may not know heaven in this life
    Still we have paradise's libation[81]
So, critic, pour me one, and sing for me
    For wine and I are siblings till my expiration:
'Should I die, bury me next to a vineyard
    'Whose roots supply my bones irrigation'[82]

The Weave of My Islam[83]

Hand me aged wine in a silver bowl[84]
Pour it despite my critics' chagrin
And drag a pouch out, as though it were
A man from Ham with arms wide open[85]
Circulate aged wine among us
That leaves my Islam finer-woven[86]
As if, when it's irked by mixing,
It were a flame before me, fervent
So pour me the thing that it contains
For it's my pleurisy's medicine
And pour her with slim, feminine midriff
Glances leaving one heartbroken
With earlocks curled above the cheeks
And pearl beads like a *lam*'s[87] flection
This is the wine I worship, which
Is also my uncles' religion[88]

O, Daughter of the Sheikh, Pour for Us[89]

O, daughter of the sheikh,[90] pour for us
Why is it your hand ceases?[91]
The water's coursed through your body
So let the wine course through us
Verily, what we imbibe –
And be not, of this, dubious –
Is all that is distinct from
The Beverage of the Virtuous[92]
Keep it far from the miser
Who makes a faith[93] of avarice
For whom Time has tarried, thus
He feels the Hour approaches[94]
Stop by the vacant campsite
And weep, if you're lugubrious
And ask the house when it was
Abandoned by its residents
We've asked it, and it's refused
To offer us responses[95]

The Vine Comes from Bounteousness[96]

Amuse yourself and a partner with wine
For therein lies rest from woe's bother
And make a morning start, for thus is
The sick man able to recover[97]
And take it, if you drink it, gleaming
With droplets from a raincloud's shower
For rain's the husband of the vineyard
So make the one the wife of the other
And pour wine not for a stingy chap
I deem it not *halal*[98] for the miser
Since the vine's from generosity[99]
The generous alone deserve its water
And take not, as your drinks partner
One feeble in reason, soiled of leather[100]
Drink, instead, with a noble gentleman
For drink behoves those of stature
Man is friend to all other men
Related, through wine, to the drinker[101]

I'm not One Who Shuns Pleasure[102]

Will you not pour your brother aged wine?
For life is in aged wine addiction
And if the reproachers reproach, I'm not
One who shuns pleasure fearing theologians[103]
It's *haram*, though its start was *halal*[104]
So let permission replace proscription
Many a slave-girl in the clothing
Of a lad; a gorgeous exhibition;[105]
Secluded, spared by her eyes of
The need for eloquence or diction;
Have I asked, once the drinkers slept, 'Won't you
'Give back the heart to him with obsession?'
She said, 'Who?' I said, 'Me', she said:
'When did you join the congregation?'
I told her, 'You've conquered my heart
'By what you've shown of *dal* and *lam* inscription'[106]
She said, 'You dozed off; whatever
'You think you saw was merely sleep's vision'

Prayer without *Takbeer*[107]

Ill-preparation left me tasting defeat
For I go about things with poor estimation
That's because I am one devoted to what
Bottles contain of pure potations
From aged wine whose shawl's of clay
Whose underwear's tar lamination
Whose radiance sparkles in the glass
Sketching masterly illustrations
As though an imaginary fancy
Were enjoying the string's intonation[108]
And one with black-and-white eyes,[109] kohl-lined
From a group of young men with initiation
At a drinks venue overlooking a tree
Whose apples smile in jubilation
With a bird perched upon a small branch
Thrilled by its fellows' exclamations
Thus passed our day, and then our night
On the roof with *tanburs*, in celebration[110]
Until we saw the darkness recede
And the sun brought the house illumination
When the time arrived for dawn prayers
We prayed, without *takbeer* proclamations[111]

Seize the Night's Remnants, and be Drunk[112]

A sincere drinks partner – nay, he adds humour
To sincerity, and is never querulous
Carrying what I make him carry, unvexed
Bearing what would irk the generous
He gave me, from the daughter of his soul,
His whole love, and shared his riches
We wandered; I in passion; he with
Generosity, for he's ever-bounteous
I called out, as we saw night whiten
As though it were dates the colour of ashes
I said, 'May the dawn see sobriety,
'My partner, in neither one of us
'Seize the night's remnants, and be drunk
'That whomever meets dawn tells, about you, stories'[113]
I acquaint him, as night recedes before us
With legions rejecting the suspicious
So when the lamp revealed what was under
The cover – the best of the vine's daughters –
He drew near, greeting one in torn clothes
Whom Fate left neither happy nor lugubrious
The vintner gifted us, when we came
A jug of wine; pierced, voluminous

From Noah's stash at the time he gathered,
        For the Ark, what was most precious
When we neared to shed its blood, its
        First hints came of scent and fragrance
As if the group's palms and what they used
        To pass it round were musk-essenced
Dawn's light didn't shine till you saw us
        Saying, with drunk heads: 'That suffices!'
You'd see us doing all that angers
        Allah – but nothing idolatrous[114]

A Cleric's Fatwa[115]

Say to the critic of the vintner's inn
And drinks by 'oud strings' fluency
That I consulted a learned cleric
Of distinguished piety
Absorbed in his faith, expert in the Law
Insightful, steeped in history
I asked: 'Is weak wine *halal*?' He said 'No
'Just strong stuff that sparks fiercely'[116]
I asked: 'What of music?' He replied:
'Only 'oud and *mizmar*[117] melodies'
I asked: 'Who should the drinks partner be?'
He said: 'Stick with idle libertines
'And strive always to be dissolute
'Seek, I urge you, the friendship of fiends'
I asked: 'And prayer?' He said: 'A must.
'Pray, but still grant wine your loyalty[118]
'Convert a year's worth of night-time prayers
'Into a daylight litany'
I asked: 'Fasting?' He said: 'Don't bother
'Eat as often as you fancy'
I asked: 'Alms-giving, and *zakat*?'[119]
He said: 'Naught but tools of villainy'

I asked: 'The Hajj pilgrimage?' He said:
'It's far away; unnecessary
'Don't go to Mecca as a pilgrim
'Even were Mecca by your garden tree'[120]
I asked: 'Tyrants?' He said: 'Don't attack them
'No matter how close their proximity[121]
'Make peace with them, and take revenge on their children
'If the infidels excite your fury
'And thrust your spear[122] in their stomachs and backs
'This is Jihad, and heaven holds glory'
I asked: 'Deposits, should they be returned?'
Him: 'Return not even date debris'[123]
'Worry instead about your debt
'With the owner of the speakeasy
'Return his deposit, and his money
'Even if it costs your last penny'
I said: 'Very well. What of a bachelor
'Travelling often, a spirit roaming free?'
He said: 'You may enjoy the pleasure
'Of a neighbour's wife, or his male progeny
'And I command you, as a duty:
'Add gambling to your repertory
'Uphold my decrees and live by them
'And I'll keep you from hell's agony'

Cease Your Reproach[124]

Cease your reproach, for reproach is but temptation
And cure me with the very cause of my debilitation[125]
Yellow-hued, no sorrow possible from it
Even in stone would it inspire elation
Poured from the palm of a girl dressed as boy
An intrigue for one of any orientation[126]
She lifts the carafe against the black night
Her face lit with brilliant radiation
Sending from the jug a stream so bright
Eyes, in its glare, close as in sedation
Wine so fine, so pure and delicate
Adding water'd be contamination
With light alone may it be mixed
Giving off dazzling illumination
Passed between lads who've humbled Time itself
So It only afflicts them with their aspirations[127]
For this do I weep, not a campsite
At which Hind and Asma' once did station[128]
God forbid Durra[129] should dwell among tents
Amid camels' and sheep's fragrant emanations
Tell, then, him who claims learning in philosophy
Knowing one thing doesn't make an education
Don't forbid forgiveness if you choose to abstain
For that forbiddance is, of faith, desecration[130]

IV

‘How Many a Tavern-Keeper I’ve Frightened…’

Visits to vintners

A Scent of Musk[1]

Pay no heed to puritanical talk
 Drink of an aromatic, restful rose
Red wine, pure, proffering its scent:
 Musk, with a hint of apple on the nose
Were it to fill the depths of a glass
 It would beam as a lantern glows
I pour again for my love, and kiss him
 Under night draped in monastic robes
Till he sings, with head inclined:
 'O for the Hanna Monastery groves'[2]

O Hanna Monastery[3]

O Hanna Monastery, where the monks dwell[4]
Who recovers from you? For I've not recovered[5]
I saw, by you, gazelles without horns[6]
Toying with our souls and natures
Be not distracted, my friend, from wine
Nor sweet basil nor indulgence in pleasure
And head to young men emaciated
By worshipping, bodies frail and slender
Whose fear of what they were warned against
Leaves them like ghosts to the observer[7]
You find them all with shaved partings[8]
Robed in worn-out frocks of leather
They don't approach water with cups, except
To add to their wine from the river

NB: Abu Hiffan tells an anecdote (Al-Mihzami, op. cit., pp. 128–30) relating to this poem, which he quotes in slightly different form, that, if at all true, would also be of pertinence to HEAD TO THE MONKS' DWELLINGS.

The story goes that when Abu Nuwas visited Egypt (some time between 805 and 807) he fell for a young Coptic Christian man, who told the poet that to attain him he must 'do whatever I tell you to'. Consenting, Abu Nuwas was thus made to wear a monk's frock, and shave 'the middle of [his] head', and wear a zunnar *(girdle worn by non-Muslims to distinguish them from Muslims), and 'become a Christian, and lampoon Islam, and praise Christianity'.*

This he did over a series of poems (one beginning: 'Many asked: What faith do you profess? I said:/ The Christian faith, for that's the truth to be followed/ A faith that permits you heavy wine drinking [...]'). And it was during Christmas Eve festivities that a buoyant Abu Nuwas began singing, 'O Hanna Monastery, where the monks dwell [...]' and the above poem followed.

'The whole time he was in Egypt', Abu Hiffan's source claims in conclusion, 'he never fasted during Ramadan, nor did he bow once in prayer except with them [i.e. the Christians]'.

Head to the Monks' Dwellings[9]

Forsake the rose and apple fields
        Head instead to the monks' dwellings[10]
Make for a group whose members have turned
        Frail as ghosts from worshipping
They repeat, as the church bells chime
        Readings from the Psalms, dusk to morning
Your ears are far from a sound you loathe
        Here you don't hear the peasant speaking[11]
But, instead, gospel lessons from books
        Talking of Christ, clarifying
How agreeable! And ancient wine in all
        Kinds of wide mugs is their offering
A slender, firm-hipped one pours for you
        With a woollen robe above his frocking

I Miss Al-Hira[12]

By God, I dearly miss
    Al-Hira,[13] and its wine
And the 'oud strings' sound at dawn
    As the church bells chime
And I miss the taverns at
    The sacrifice time[14]
And spending, on drink and
    Beardless youths, my every dime
By God, were you to hear
    The poems I've devised
Their splendour would leave you in
    Despair till your demise

A Vintner's Tavern in Anbar[15]

Nicer than a campsite in Dhu Qar[16]
    Is a vintner's tavern in Anbar[17]
And the smell of sweet basil, and narcissi
    Is finer than saddled camels, by far
And intimacy with gentle maidens
    And a young gazelle wrapped in *zunnar*[18]
Are more pleasant than a tiring desert
    And the mirage's cruel canard
Reverberations of an ʿoud, plucked
    By the fingertips of perfumed young stars
Are better, to me, than Umm Najiya
    And Umm ʿAmr, and Umm ʿAmmar[19]

NB: Al-Isfahani writes that Abu Nuwas was with Muslim ibn al-Walid, who was reciting poetry 'rhapsodising about the deserts' and their bucolic tranquillity, until Abu Nuwas 'grew irritated listening to it' and recited the above poem.

How Lovely is a Karkh Bar[20]

May the day never come that God destroys Karkh
Nor Susa's convivial parlours[21]
How lovely is a Karkh bar, that gathers us
Where we follow, with drinks, Lucifer
Radiant wine, red, crystal-clear
Aged in Karkh by Qadoos, its vintner[22]
Of different faith,[23] with grey hair locks
Greeted both by rabbi and minister
Once the wine turns clear, he lets flow
A red draught, driving off displeasure
Brought by one with two fine, bright cheeks
Matching the Queen of Sheba's splendour
Dressed in *kurta*, and Khorasani clothes[24]
By God, none's like him in Toos, nor Merv[25]

Many a Vintner I've Come to, Unguided[26]

Many a vintner I've come to, unguided
Except by royal Persian wine bouquets
And he's opened the door in fright, to
Night as black as *taylasan*[27] drapes
Yet, when he saw the wine pouch before me
He spoke as one no longer afraid:
'Of Tameem?'[28] I said: 'Not at all!
'From Yemen do I originate'[29]
He took the spigot and pierced the cask
Round and hefty as a camel's waist
Bringing forth a flame, casting
From the Euphrates to Oman its blaze
I've seen that things, when preserved, improve
Yet wine, when preserved, depreciates[30]
Except in colour, and clarity of skin
Its soul remaining, though its body wastes

The Abandoned Tavern[31]

A drinking house, neglected and abandoned
Traces of past life still marked
Grooves of wine pouches dragged on its soil
And basil bouquets, some moist, some parched
I shut my friends in, that they'd rejuvenate
And I was there with them from the start
And it was as if they were the same
Men seen in East Sabat's desert parts[32]
We spent a day, then another, then a third
And not until the fifth did we depart
Wine circulated in a gilded bowl
Adorned with colourful Persian art
On the base a Khosrow, and on the sides
An oryx speared by horsemen's darts
Wine was poured up to their necks
Then water up to their hats' marks

NB: As mentioned in the introduction, this poem is one of Abu Nuwas' more sophisticated lampoons of the desert 'traces' (atlal) *motif. Rather than the usual exhortation against weeping at the lover's former campsite, here the campsite is replaced by a dilapidated wine tavern, and mourned with mock-seriousness. The renowned essayist al-Jahith (d. 869) is said to have particularly liked this poem, telling his nephew Yamut ibn al-Muzarra', 'I know of no poetry better than [this]' (according to al-Isfahani).*

If I am a Reprobate[33]

If I am a reprobate, debauched
To whose mind occurs no piety
Then those of restraint, and rectitude
Have paid, for the praise of men, highly
Money stains not men of noble honour
So my honour's preserved with money
I love the mellow wild cow calf[34]
And hide not this love, and so he flees
I began early at the wine parlour
Where the tap stabbed the cask's belly
At which a vein spewed over its chest
Like an anklet's curve in trajectory
Then it filled up a stoppered jug
Unleashing pearl sellers' commodity[35]
I addressed the Devil, and said to him
'Pour not for those who reproach me'
Then I was served, along with my friend
Wine mixed with water, fresh, pristine

How did You Get to My Harem?[36]

Many's the vintner I've found at night
Camels tired by journeying far
And he's spluttered; torpor in his eyes
Like a drunk wearing the hangover's scars:
'How did you get to my harem
'While the night's star is kohled with tar?'
I said: 'Calm down, I just spotted
'Dawn's light shine in amongst the barns'
In reply he uttered: 'Dawn?
'There's none but the glow of the wine jar'
He rose and plugged the mouth of the cask
And night was once again clothed in char
Then he unleashed the bung in a cup
The sides and base of which were carved
Depicting, at the bottom, Khosrow
And on the sides his martial guard
A mass of troops beneath his stirrups
In tunics, waving flag spars

NB: Sidqi recounts a story attributed to Sulayman ibn Nawbakht in relation to this poem. Sulayman had persuaded Abu Nuwas to agree to accompany him to Mecca for the Hajj, on the latter's condition that they pass by Tiyzanabad en route. There Abu Nuwas 'called on a vintner he knew well, named Sirjis, and drank day and night', at one point reciting the above poem. 'And he didn't stop [this routine] until the first pilgrims passed by us, and made their pilgrimage, and then returned, at which point we departed with them to Baghdad as though we had done the Hajj with them' (Alhan al-Han, *pp. 41–2).*

How Many a Tavern-Keeper I've Frightened[37]

How many a tavern-keeper I've frightened
Waking him while he's wrapped in his sheets
His dogs have come to know the night-travellers
And so they keep a distance from the street[38]
I scanned all the other establishments
Before entering his property
I spotted him, through the night's darkness
By his beard's grey, and his bald spot's sheen
O tavern-keeper, don't be afraid
For the banned drink is the same as the clean[39]
So leave that which your hands pressed, and
Give me, God praise you, wine of the feet[40]
That which the traders chose, producing
A sting on tasting like pepper's pique
And it creeps through the bones, when taken
With the tongue, like the onset of sleep
Their palms were perfumed by it, as though
They held a necklace of carnation beads
A palm pours it for you, beloved
Whether with generosity or greed[41]
So I emulated the proverb-like
Line from the master Hassan's[42] poetry:
'That which you gave me and I returned
'Was killed, damn you, so get me one that breathes'[43]

A Friend of Moses[44]

One of blazing cheeks and bewitching glance
Whose looks are like full moon's shine
When he walks, he shakes from his throat
All down his sides till his hip's incline
And his steps, when he shows off his rear
While he walks, are but inches at a time
I called at night on a tavern keeper
Of wasted limbs, and stooped spine
He brought one out, dragging it, as if
It were a corpse, or one risen from a shrine
He drew his cheek close to the carafes' rims
And guffawed in delight at the wine
Then poured it, and mixed it, then were written
Eight letter *waws* laughing in a line[45]
I said, 'Wine, how many years have you?'
She said, 'I lived an age in the cask, confined'
I said, 'Khosrow held you?' She scowled
Saying, 'Your impatience leaves you behind
'I knew Moses, the friend of Khidr[46]
'And heard of Dhul-Qarnayn before his decline[47]
'And, were I immortal, I'd live therein
'Till unto Judgment Day I were consigned'
Thus we stayed, frowning at the wine's burn
As the Devil urged us on with drunken rhymes

Tell Us, Wine, How many Years have You?[48]

I took pleasure in wine, and revelry
And the preserved home of a Persian seigneur
With some trusty youths, heads of Banu Malik[49]
And the lofty Azd Oman[50] of great lustre
We alighted by a man of greying hair
Kind-faced, clearly a non-believer
His was the priest's faith; secretary's rigour
A stooping giant, poetic orator
He greeted us, saying: 'Do come in!
'To welcome you is our utmost pleasure'
We told him, 'Aged wine's our nourishment
'And we're men of reason and mental vigour
'Will you then pour us wine old enough
'To recall the tales of Persia's emperors?'
He brought one out, body ravaged by time
Pained by the midday heat of summer
I said to her when her brilliance shone
On the cup's surface, in my raised fingers:
'Tell us, wine, how many years have you?'
She said, 'God rebuke you, I can't remember
'I saw Thamud[51] when their decline set in
'And I knew the days of 'Amr ibn 'Amer'[52]

We were poured by one of slender face
    With the rogue's snort, and lover's swagger
We persisted in this nourishment
    For thirty days one after another
Indulging in all that God despises
    But belief in other than Lord of al-Masha'ir[53]

A Jewish Winemaker[54]

I led a large group riding till noon
When we stopped at a vintner's marquee
Seeing by his girdle he wasn't Muslim[55]
We thought of him well, but he was wary
We asked, 'Of the faith of Jesus, son of Mary?'
He turned in disgust, and cursed obscenely
A Jew, therefore, who appears to like you
And conceals from you his infidelity
We asked, 'What's your name?' He said: 'Samuel
'Though I go by Abu 'Amr falsely
'An Arab name that's done me no good
'Brought me neither status nor glory
'Its letters, at least, are light and few
'Unlike others, though it's not burden free'
We said, amazed at his mellifluous tongue:
'You impress us; may your wine do equally'
He turned away once more, then glanced at
Our legs, then faces alternately
And said, 'If you'd said that to someone else
'They'd reproach you, though I'll show clemency'[56]
Then he brought a golden, oily wine
As we lay prostrate, impatiently

So great was it, we stayed for thirty days
Even though we'd only set out for three
An awful group, none like them in an age
And I was among them; don't exempt me
Were the time for prayer to approach
They would shoo it away, drunkenly

NB: Abu Hiffan recounts an anecdote (Al-Mihzami, op. cit., pp. 42–7) about this poem, incorporating also the poem I'M FREED OF THE IMAM'S REPROACH. *It holds that the Caliph al-Amin was once angry with Abu Nuwas, for he was eager to drink with him, but had been unable to get hold of him for several days. He dispatched people to search the bars, and other places where he was ordinarily to be found, but with no luck. Other drinking partners, who 'envied Abu Nuwas' status with [al-Amin]', began disparaging him, telling the caliph the poet was 'a scoundrel, a boor, a vulgar companion of despicable people and riffraff', whose company was 'an abomination to the Commander of the Believers'. This further annoyed al-Amin, who snapped back, 'There could be no more suitable drinks partner for a caliph than one of his refinement, and charm, and knowledge'.*

When he was finally found, it was in a Jew's tavern, where he was said to have spent a solid month of hard drinking. Summoned before the furious caliph, Abu Nuwas was warned that if he was spotted drinking in any tavern ever again he would be executed. Thus, for an ensuing time period, al-Amin didn't see the poet, who in turn obeyed the order of abstinence, until a day came when the caliph 'had a morning drink […] and relaxed, and recalled Abu Nuwas, and the pleasure of his company, and the brilliance of his conversation, and the rarity of everything about him', and ordered for him to be summoned.

When the contrite poet arrived, the caliph asked him to 'recite what you have said about your time there [i.e. in the Jewish tavern]', and so he began, 'I led a large group riding till noon [...]'. After he finished the poem, a pleased al-Amin told his servant to pour drinks for everyone present except Abu Nuwas. When the poet asked why, the caliph replied, 'Because you describe the young man, when he hands you the glass, as pouring you two glasses; a glass with his eyes, and a glass with his hand. And you mention your flirtation with him, so give us now what you might say if he didn't pour for you'. Thus Abu Nuwas began, 'Critic, I'm freed of the Imam's reproach [...]'.

And when he was finished, al-Amin said, 'Damn you, there's no deliverance from you at all! Young man, pour for him!'

Don't Pour in Secret[57]

Will you not pour me wine, and tell me, 'This is wine'?!
Don't pour in secret when you can do it openly[58]
And don't pour the hypocrites one single drop
For hypocrisy to me's obscenity
The young man's life is drunkenness after drunkenness
Time is short for those who drink lengthily
What is loss but that you find me sober?
What's gain but the stir of inebriety?
Say the name of your love, and spare me pseudonyms
There's no good in cloaked felicity
Nor in decadence without ribaldry
Nor in ribaldry without disbelief
A forehead like a crescent, surrounded by
Stars adorns each man of revelry
Many a vintner I've woken from slumber
When Altair vanished and Gemini was seen[59]
And she asked, 'Who're the visitors?' And we said:
'A group light of drink pouches; thirsty;
'Who *must* copulate'. She said, 'How about
'One bright as dinars, eyes droopy?
'Enjoyed alike by the philanderer, and
'The one who takes pleasure in sodomy'[60]

We said, 'Bring him! For him, in our state,
    'We'd offer up our own family'
So she brought him, twig-slender, swaggering
    You'd think him a creature of sorcery
With a brassy sheen like the full moon's
    Svelte above the hip, white in the teeth
We went to him one after another
    And broke the fast of our celibacy
We became in God's eyes the worst men
    Dragging sin's hems, but not boastfully[61]

The Hilltop Tent[62]

Many a guard's[63] tent sits atop a hill
        Those climbing it fear their hands stumble
It's in shade if the sun's at its back
        But entry, when sunlit, is possible
We dumped our luggage there, wrecked by the heat
        Of a Sirius noon, a wickless candle[64]
It tarried somewhat, then brought a measure
        Of shade; a ragged lodging, feeble
As though we were between wings of an ostrich
        Raising its chest above the bed of the camel[65]
I milked, for my friends, the east wind's rain[66]
        With the groves' water's wine, scent-filled
Should it pass beneath the lad's uvula
        His worries would announce withdrawal
When night brought darkness, I was childish
        Seeing beauty in the non-beautiful
I unleashed myself between the helper's loins
        Though he, as friend, was unparalleled
So I blamed the drink; how beneficent it is[67]
        And how its beneficence to you is a toll
I gave my love forthright conversation
        Subdued one who'd not been pliable
He sang, while my hand was his cheek's pillow:
        'Might I have sought the unobtainable?[68]

'It's sad enough when the kind are stingy
'And no miser is charitable'[69]
I'll seek wealth, either drinking with a caliph
Or as a terroriser of the trail
With every lad whose heart won't falter
When the soldiers call out the names of the felled
Thus we'd take God's fifth from every sinner[70]
Gluttonous, profligate with life's frills
Don't you see this money aids piety, and[71]
A miser isn't like a giving wastrel?[72]

NB: The poet, litterateur, prince, and one-day caliph Ibn al-Mu'tazz (d. 908) recounts a story pertaining to this poem in his Tabaqat al-Shu'ra' *('The Classes of Poets'), sourced ultimately to the Basran scholar al-Asma'i (d. 828). It goes that, during the Harun years, al-Asma'i was once hosted by two of the Barmakids – the powerful vizier Yahya ibn Khalid and his son al-Fadhl – for a lavish meal. After eating food 'the enjoyment and deliciousness of which was unmatched by anything in the world I'd ever had, whether with a caliph or a king', the group was served wine. No sooner had al-Asma'i's first sip passed his lips before 'I almost flew in happiness and delight, and the pleasure left me as though in the skin of a twenty-year-old. And the drink crept in and softened all between the hair and the sole of the foot [...] and I couldn't restrain myself from exclaiming, "God damn Abu Nuwas for his saying: "Should it pass beneath the lad's uvula/ His worries would announce withdrawal"!"'.*

At which al-Fadhl asked al-Asma'i if he could recite the entire poem. When he did, al-Fadhl cried out, 'God damn him, how poetic he was!' And then: 'By God, were it not for what the people said about him, I wouldn't be apart from him, yet if I think about him I find him a man ribald, dissolute, shameless, addicted to the vintners' taverns'. To which al-Asma'i replied, 'And yet, despite that, he's a man of refined standing; I have sat with him at many gatherings, attended by all kinds of litterateurs and scholars, and there was nothing of their arts with which he couldn't keep pace; indeed he surpassed them'.

*To reinforce his point, al-Asma'i then recited one of Abu Nuwas' panegyrics for Yahya himself. To which Yahya replied, 'As I said, were it not for his debauchery, I would never leave his company' (*Tabaqat al-Shu'ra'*, pp. 213–17).*

V

'You, Finest Company a Drinker Could Keep'

Toasts to friends (and financiers)

It was Evening, and He was Sober[1]

They squinted, astonished, at the drinks partner
For it was evening, and he was sober
Only one attempt is necessary
To waken him from drunken slumber
And he doesn't say, 'No! Leave me'
Or ask, 'What is it you're after?'
But rather, 'Pour me', adding too:
'Make it straight if you've no water'
When noon strikes, he goes to pray
Though he skips afternoon and night prayer
Those he prays at the other's time
Always completing what's required[2]
That's Muhammad,[3] I offer him my soul
As he deserves – and how paltry's the offer

NB: Abu Hiffan tells a story about this poem (op. cit., pp. 114–6), narrated by a Yusuf ibn al-Daya. Al-Amin was having a glass one morning with Abu Nuwas and some others when he proposed they imbibe away the entire day, 'that we may see which of us is the best at drinking'. So they drank until late in the night, when all had slept except Abu Nuwas. After a short nap himself, Abu Nuwas went to wake al-Amin, saying, 'O Commander of the Believers, you have withheld from us the fair treatment with which you customarily favour your flock, and you have left me to drink alone'.

At this al-Amin arose, telling the poet, 'Damn you, you have cost yourself a pleasure greater than your indulgence of this drink'. Abu Nuwas asked what that was, to which he said, 'Sleep, in which the body's components are righted, and through which it finds balance'.

'My sir', said Abu Nuwas, 'the pleasure of this drink takes the place of that sleep'.

So they drank away the remainder of the night until dawn broke, at which point al-Amin wanted to sleep. Abu Nuwas told him to listen to some lines he'd prepared, and then recited the above poem. Afterward, al-Amin said, 'By God, bravo!' and ordered his servant Kawthar to pay the poet 'a thousand dirhams[4] for each line'.

To which Abu Nuwas said, 'That is the rightful value of the lines, but what about my beating you all at drinking?'

Al-Amin told him to name his sum, which he put at a further thousand dirhams. 'And what will you do with it?' asked al-Amin. 'My sir, I will head this morning to al-Karkh, which I left several days ago, and wander its gardens, and drink and be dissolute, and then return'.

'Kawthar', said al-Amin, 'give him [the dirhams], and may God not bless him!'

Wake Your Drinks Partner[5]

Wake your drinks partner, for he's dozed off
That he, in dark, may fill your beaker
Pure, unmixed, as though its radiance
Were coal in the palm of the drinker
From an orchard selected, and sown
In 'Ana[6] by a Persian emperor
So powerful it leaves the tongue
Of the young lad tied and unheard
He's called for, so raises his head
And, once left alone, it falters
You're poured by one *kurta*-clad
Hurrying those slow with the pitcher[7]
With soft eyelids, as though he were
The gardens' gazelle in slumber
The Imam Muhammad[8] has shone a light
For the faith bright as glowing ember
The caliphate's already seen five
How fortunate the sixth came after[9]
Full moons weep at his chuckle
And swords cackle when he's bothered[10]

NB: Ibn al-Mu'tazz recounts a story (op. cit., pp. 209–11) related to this poem, traced ultimately to Abu Hiffan. Al-Amin, it says, had

*had a new sitting area (*majlis*) built, 'the likes of which neither Arab nor foreigner had ever seen'; emblazoned with artwork; its ceiling, walls, and doors gilded; its curtains and other furniture handsomely dyed and also gilded. Upon its completion, the caliph invited 'drinking partners and poets', including Abu Nuwas, over one morning for an all-day party. Being told by al-Amin to 'not spoil my pleasure with coyness, nor ruin my delight with reserve, but [to] be merry', the company ate and then drank wine 'whose aroma was more delicious than the scent of a lover' until the late night, when all had fallen asleep except Abu Nuwas, who continued to drink alone. At the point just before daybreak (*al-sahar*), Abu Nuwas awoke the caliph, saying, 'O Master of the Worlds, do you not see the fineness of this breeze, and the excellence of this northerly wind, and the coolness of this* sahar, *and the perfection of this air, and the serene atmosphere, and the magnificence of this light?'*

To which al-Amin sat up and replied, 'Abu Nuwas, I am able neither to drink nor to stay awake, but your prose description has pleased me; therefore invigorate me with your drinking poetry'. So Abu Nuwas recited the above poem, after which al-Amin 'relaxed' and began imbibing once again.

He Sipped It with the Sipper[11]

The inebriate turned his eyes
        Abstaining from the beaker
Yet, when he feared harassment
        From companions and sitters[12]
And knew they'd accept no plea
        He sipped it with the sipper
From the palms of a languid-eyed
        Dulcet flirt, with a swagger
Scheduling appointments with us
        With his eyes, and forehead flickers
While you may be named ʿAbbas
        You're not one to glower[13]
At munificence; instead you
        Frown when others suffer[14]
With al-Fadhl, you take precedence,
        O, Abul-Fadhl, over all others[15]

NB: This poem offers further insight into the means by which poets earned their living. It's already been stated in the introduction that, before Abu Nuwas was able to secure the patronage of the Caliph al-Amin, he depended on the largesse of the Nawbakht clan. Here we see another prominent family that could evidently be relied on to provide supplementary income in exchange for public praise. Wagner's Diwan *contains no fewer than seven panegyrics for this al-'Abbas, seventeen for his father al-Fadhl, two for al-Fadhl's brother Ja'far, and two for another of al-Fadhl's sons, Muhammad. The poem also demonstrates again how Abu Nuwas consistently blended genres – as with his panegyrics for al-Amin (cf.* IT WAS EVENING, AND HE WAS SOBER; WAKE YOUR DRINKS PARTNER*), he can't resist incorporating the wine theme, praising his patron for his judicious appreciation of drink.*

Anbar Wine[16]

The ruined abode is mute, reserved
Silenced, and deprived of speech
A vexed lover lent it his
Dumbfoundedness when he saw his sweet
It's no wonder that a trace[17] should
Shun a crazed lover, starved of sleep
An aromatic, musky wine
Housed in al-Anbar or Heet[18]
As though it were, when mixed, the sun
Dwelling in Aries or Pisces[19]
Or the full moon's halo, rising
On day fourteen, precisely[20]
As if it were that, or, instead
The face of ʻAbbas[21] in beauty
Or rather, his face has its beauty
For it's of pearls and rubies[22]

The Finest Company a Drinker Could Keep[23]

Coyness caught the tongue of a fellow rake
        From his lips issued not a peep
When I turned my gaze to his face
        I found his eyelids fastened in sleep
Shaking him, I said, 'Wake up
        'You, finest company a drinker could keep
'That I may banish your woes with a glass
        'And lift your spirits off this heap'
He replied, voice enfeebled by drink
        With dawn's first light beginning to seep:
'I understand, but from wine strong as this
        'The path to recovery's too steep'

A Safeguard against the Caprice of Time[24]

A friend whose company was adornment
Of Yemeni roots, if he assigned[25]
A great man of exalted qualities
Spending the wildest sums on wine
A full moon in darkness, rain to arid soil
Eager to grant favours, endlessly kind
An urbane, well-bred, noble man
A safeguard against the caprice of Time[26]
Prisoner of love, slain by pretty women
Shedding the reins,[27] keeping the glass inclined
I called to him, while the night was veiled
And dawn's bright spot was yet to shine:
'Come, dear friend, to aged wine, that we may
'Drive the legions of sorrow to decline'[28]
He didn't reply except with a stammer
Even, to the brightest lad, mystifying
I kept distracting him with incantations
Till sleep's barrier was raised from his mind
And he, in pleasure, broke out in song:
'Wind, what do you do with desert lines?'[29]

Take It to Banish Suffering[30]

Forget the traces of dwellings and remains[31]
        And forgo the residence left empty
Have you ever seen the dwellings reply
        In answer to him who queries?
Drink that, like the eye of a rooster,[32]
        Whose taste repels woe and enmity[33]
One that would, if plunged in my veins
        Have woe fleeing my heart hurriedly
Many a most noble drinking partner
        Who goes, wherever you go, gladly
Is dizzied by the cups of straight draught
        Till he's thrown to forehead off his feet
I said, when dawn's first signs appeared
        And tore the hems of night's obscurity:
'Come, I'll rid you of all unpleasantness
        'Have a morning draught, aged, perfumy'
He bemoaned the force of his hangover
        And was, in taking the glass, tardy
I said, 'Take it to banish suffering
        'For it brings hangovers fatality'
So he sat up straight, revealing a hand
        Whose palm had not yet set the glass free
And sang, after imbibing three sips:
        'Restrain the eye from crying for debris'[34]

Disregard Him who Rebukes It[35]

I said, once morning emerged
        And kindled effulgently
And the stars' last trace slipped
        Behind the horizon's seam
And I saw the rooster crowing
        At the dawn repeatedly,
To Abu Bishr, my dear friend
        Wherever he may journey:
This is wine, openly
        So don't drink it secretly
Not like one who euphemises
        In fear of ignominy
And drink none but the bitter finest
        Expelling anxiety
Like the musk whose scent wafts
        From ambergris perfumery
Leaving man, if he tastes it
        In comfortable drapery
Seeing daytime as nighttime
        And Friday as Saturday[36]
Disregard him who rebukes it
        And insists on chastity

Drinking water in wine's place
        Menial and lowly
And keep it from Abu Ayyub[37]
        When he swaggers proudly
He sold strong wine for weak draught[38]
        There's a losing industry
Like a buyer of thoroughbreds
        Who prefers, to horse, donkey

VI

'I Ran with Youthful Passion Like a Wild Horse'

Autobiographical fragments

I Hear You, Leader of the Believers, and Obey[1]

'Lend your poetry to foregone remains[2]
    'Your wine depictions have done enough damage'
A sovereign[3] forced me to describe remains
    My arm, when I gave the order, took umbrage
I hear you, Leader of the Believers,[4] and obey
    Though you burden me with a rough voyage

I don't Taste the Wine Except by Nose[5]

You who are setting out to rebuke, rebuke!
        I don't taste the wine except by nose
I was censured for it by an *imam*[6]
        Whom I wouldn't deem it right to oppose
So pass it to another, for I'm not
        Its companion except in prose[7]
The extent of my share, if it's passed round
        Is to see it, smelling what the air blows
It's as if I am, when extolling it,
        One extolling the *tahkeem*[8] in repose
Fatigued by carrying weapons of war
        Asking the fit that he be deposed

NB: Abu Hiffan recounts a lengthy vignette (Al-Mihzami, op. cit., pp. 119–124) relating to this poem and the one below, SPARE ME FROM KHURAFA'S SAYINGS. *A man called Abul-Khayr hosted a gathering whose attendees included Abu Nuwas; a stableman of Harun's named Dufafa al-'Ansi; and an unnamed songstress with 'the finest face and singing voice, without parallel in Baghdad'. They had lunch, enjoying a wine 'whose like', according to the storyteller, 'Ali ibn Khassa, 'I had never seen in purity and fineness'. During the meal Ibn Khassa teased Abu Nuwas, saying, 'Damn you, drink with us, don't force on your soul an abstinence to which it isn't accustomed'. But the poet declined, protesting, 'There is no way [I can do] that', and then recited the above verse.*

After lunch, however, Abul-Khayr brought out a slave girl, who had 'a face the likes of whose beauty, perfect splendour, and flawless proportion we had never seen, leaving us bewildered and flabbergasted'. She sat near Abu Nuwas and joked flirtatiously with him, lightening his spirits, then brought out an 'oud and started playing it, before singing with 'a voice that stole our hearts and minds'. After a dance, during which Ibn Khassa 'saw Abu Nuwas' knee [touching] the knee of [the woman]', they went back to the sitting area for more wine. Abu Nuwas then recited a poem in praise of the woman, concluding with a call for a toast of drinks to her voice.

This prompted them to enquire if he himself would be participating in the toast. His response was to ask the woman if she would recite a poem, which she did, playing the 'oud with it: 'If you don't love, or know of passion/ Then be stone, rock-dry, petrified/ For what is life but pleasure and desire/ Even if haters rebuke and decry it'.

At this Abu Nuwas 'shouted a cry that shook the house, and said: "By God, well done! May God curse him who fears Muhammad [al-Amin]! I must have a measure [of drink], even if it leads to my beheading!"' He then drank three measures in quick succession, and recited SPARE ME FROM KHURAFA'S SAYINGS *(below).*

After that, he said to the group: 'Keep my secret, for I drank, and disobeyed and lampooned [the caliph], and if [you don't] it'll be the end of our relationship'. They assured him they would, at which he said, 'Pass round measures vigorously', and they drank the night away till dawn.

Spare Me from Khurafa's Sayings[9]

Pour for me, and for Dhufafa
O, Abul-Khayr, a wine serving[10]
And pour the head of charm and fun
To the luck of bird-releasing[11]
Wine of pomp and haughtiness
Kept safe from wrongdoing
Other than me's who disdains her
Out of fear, or hoping[12]
Give me her openly, and spare me
From Khurafa's sayings[13]
Those who harmed her went astray,
O Dhufafa, and faced a humbling
Just as the caliphate, after Harun
Was left humbled, and straying[14]

I'm Freed of the Imam's Reproach[15]

Critic, I'm freed of the Imam's reproach[16]
And I've expressed what was deep in my mind
I told our pourer, 'Take it away', for I can't
Defy the Believers' Commander[17] and drink wine
He's forbidden me wine that sends up
To the heavens, like a tent rope, its shine[18]
If the drinker gulped it, you'd think he was
Kissing a planet in the depth of nighttime
You see, wherever it is in the house, sunrise
And, where it isn't, the sun's decline
A nasal-voiced pourer brings it around
Earlocks curled like a scorpion's spine
He poured them, his eyes giving me desire
Which, to my heart, was more pleasant, and more fine[19]

NB: Abu Hiffan tells a story pertaining in part to this poem; *see* A JEWISH WINEMAKER.

I Sought Pleasure in Qutrabbul[20]

I sought pleasure in Qutrabbul, coming
With hard currency reserves, loaded
Eighty good dinars[21] I'd saved up
And spent them all till I drank on credit
I sold a fine shirt, and outer garment
And a robe with sides decorated
To a vintner of Ibn 'Imran's[22] faith
Called Umm Husain; sophisticated
I said, 'If you aren't generous with a
'Gift, then I must have a face-kiss'
She said, 'Might you prefer instead
'A beardless lad, dinar-eyed, languid?'
She fetched him, his face a bright full moon
Nasal-voiced, tender, buttocks solid
I had come to Qutrabbul laden
With ample cargo, heavy-weighted
Yet I left impoverished, not at all rich[23]
Out of pocket to the tune of two hundred
The vintner told me on departure
Once the wine left me Hunain-footed:[24]
'May you live in beauty wherever you go'
And I left, when I did, humiliated

NB: This poem is said to recount Abu Nuwas' return journey from Egypt to Baghdad in c. 806–7. Al-Isfahani tells the story as follows: on his way back from Egypt, the poet passed by Homs, which impressed him with 'the multitude of its vintners, and the non-restraint of its drinkers', so he spent a number of days imbibing there 'morning and evening', some of which time was in the company of a Jewish winemaker named Levi (Arabic Lawi*). The latter told him, 'Our drink is better than the drink of Qutrabbul', to which Abu Nuwas replied, 'Were it not for the purity of the drink of Qutrabbul, and its riding of the nape of the Tigris' neck, it would not be but a single one of your taverns!'*

He then left Homs for Iraq. Arriving at al-Anbar, he decided he couldn't enter Baghdad without having paid a visit to Qutrabbul, where he proceeded to spend all his remaining money, forcing him to sell his clothes, whence the inspiration for the above poem.

Another poem; a panegyric addressed to Harun; is also said by some commentators to allude to this same return journey; see CRACKS IN THE HEAVENS.

Cracks in the Heavens[25]

I wept a long time at the houses' traces[26]
Repeatedly pained in abundance
As if I were hunting a game animal
Seen in front, then behind the next moment[27]
So when despair set in, I steered my camel
Away, and comfort took precedence
To a tavern where the dogs don't growl[28]
At me, nor oppose my long residence
Thus I didn't leave till all that my hand
Held was gone, even shoes and garments
But if the wine took my inherited funds
It didn't take my shame or benevolence
Many a glass like the sky's lamp I drank
Over a kiss, or romantic appointments
Of wine aged till it became as though
Light slipping through cracks in the heavens[29]
You'd see its glare from outside the glass
To hide its rim wouldn't shield its brilliance
God bless the one who governed events ably
And gave Harun, of the caliphs, preeminence
We live well as long as we're pious and
Our world's under his governance
An *imam* who so fears God, it's as if
He expects, any moment, His appearance

Haughty, with long forearms, as though
He needs a banner to tie his scabbards[30]

NB: The above is one of Abu Nuwas' five formal panegyrics addressed to the Caliph Harun al-Rashid. While readers of this book might find it strange to see the poet writing so solemnly about 'piety' and 'fearing God', the reaction from medieval commentators was quite the opposite: the grammarian and critic al-Mubarrad (d. 898) was astonished that he dared speak so explicitly about wine and romance in a poem addressed to the famously stern caliph in person at his court. 'I know of no one who praised a caliph and [incorporated such themes]', al-Isfahani quotes him as saying.

*The poem is also believed by some to have been delivered upon Abu Nuwas' return from Egypt (c. 806/7), as a sort of olive branch extended to the ruler with whom the poet had never had an easy time. The reference to his drinking away all his money and even his clothes certainly calls to mind another poem composed about this return journey (*I SOUGHT PLEASURE IN QUTRABBUL*), though the notion that it was the Barmakids who arranged his appearance in court – as al-Isfahani's source asserts – is nonsensical since, as P. Kennedy points out (*A Genius of Poetry*, p. 83), the Barmakids had been violently banished from Harun's administration several years previously. The same source's claim that Harun awarded the poet twenty thousand dirhams[31] for the poem also seems incredible, given we know the caliph was in foul spirits generally by the time Abu Nuwas returned to Baghdad, and indeed would jail the poet shortly afterward. Nonetheless, the reference to the caliph in the eleventh line as 'Abu al-Umana'' ('The Father of al-Amin, al-Ma'mun, and al-Mu'tamin') does suggest the occasion was in the final decade of*

Harun's reign,[32] *and, allowing for embellishment and chronological confusion on the grapevine (so to speak), the basic outline of the story doesn't seem especially implausible. A second panegyric addressed to Harun (Wagner,* Diwan, *Book I, p. 106) is also said to have been composed upon the poet's return from Egypt, this time – more plausibly – on the advice of the Nawbakhts.*

A Wild Horse[33]

I ran with youthful passion like a wild horse
And the choice of wickedness came easy
I found the most pleasant loan of the nights
Was the tune paired with the string's fluency
And a songstress, who'd sing, if desired:
'When were the tents in Dhu Tuloohi?'[34]
Enjoy youth that shall not endure
And join morn's drink with that of the eve
Take dark, rubicund wine, so bright
The miser'd pay his finest milk as its fee
Selected for a Khosrow by his scouts
Fortunate twice: in taste and pungency
Don't you see I've spent my honour in wine
And the bite of lips of the fair *dhabi*?[35]
And I'm aware that the distance shall
Be great between my soul and body

NB: Al-Isfahani writes that the critic al-Hasan ibn Abi Riyah 'used to marvel' at this last line, saying, 'If you want, you can make it the speech of a determined libertine, indifferent to what [sins] he has committed; and [equally] if you want, you can make it the speech of someone seeking repentance as he faces death'.

Youth was the Riding-camel of Ignorance[36]

Youth was the riding-camel of ignorance
        And the embellisher of laughs and joking
It was beautiful, if I chose to wear it
        And walked, with noisy sandals, strutting
It was eloquent, if I spoke with it
        Ears were lent when I was talking
It was the intercessor in desires
        With the girls, and knew aching[37]
And the stimulant, once people slept
        So I was, after the husband, following[38]
And the commander; even were my spirit
        Resolved, it brought my hands to doing
Now, though, I've taken my saddlebag
        Off youth's back, and my step's lost its spring
And wine's my love, even if it robs me
        Of livelihood, and drains my savings
Yellow wine, acclaimed by Persian rulers
        Too great for comparing or likening
Preserved for Adam before his creation
        Thus, by a previous step, preceding
A thing has come to you that you cannot feel
        But by instinctive reasoning

The eye wanders over its skin
    Like the finest leaf, smooth, gleaming
If water raises it, it clothes it
    In bubbles like anklet bells, jingling
Until, once its turmoil's calmed
    It creates, like ants' legs, writing
Two lines, part scattered, part conjoined
    In script without dots or vowelling[39]
Forgive your brother, then, for he's a man
    Whose ears have grown used to reproaching

Pouring for Baghdad, and the Days[40]

Pouring for Baghdad, and the days
        When our time was spent in play
With young men like the night's stars
        Never vulgar for one day
Their crowns were clemency; pouring brought out
        Their generous and charming ways
From their glances came suns, which
        No description could portray
Poured by one of black-and-white eyes;[41]
        Flowing earlock; languid gaze
Burring the letter 'R', in such[42]
        A way that brings mortal decay
Should he wish to hurry, his rump would stop him
        If he bent down, his legs would give way[43]
He pours them a bright red ruby
        Blazing, in hand, like a lamp's ray
At times, they were given it mixed
        Or straight at another stage
Till inebriety threw him to his face
        And the hidden was on display
Then he began to sing, merrily
        While on the verge of standing straight:
'How the eyes' seeping kindles
        'When the lover's face goes away'

The Mosque has Vanished[44]

The mosque has vanished; the dunes are deserted
As Labab and the Mirbads are empty[45]
The mosque that combined *virtus* and
Religion's gone, with its courts and lobbies[46]
Places I frequented as a lad
Until white hairs grew on my cheeks
Among youths like swords, brandished
In life's prime, decked with decency
Then Time worked its caprice, and they were
Scattered to the winds across countries
Time will never beget others like them
For me – Never! – they were unique
When I grew certain their departure
Wouldn't be undone as long as I breathed
My patience was tested like no other's
And I was torn by myriad needs
Likewise were I to lose a brother
We'd no longer share fraternity[47]
My mother's now the grape;[48] Qutrabbul's
My spring home; Karkh's the summer sanctuary
She[49] nurses me with her milk, shading
Me from the blaze of midday heat
When her twigs fold together, I'm
Entirely covered; there's no breach

While doves spend the night, as if
        At a funeral, wailing with the bereaved
Our desires[50] rise up together
        As though taken by ecstasy
So I begin to crawl to her milk
        Like a hungry child struggling to its feet
Till I select a tavern's daughter
        Aged for years till maturity
I tore from her, while night was dark,
        Fabric, woven fine, hem-free[51]
By a clumsy seamstress, who used neither
        Cord nor tent rope during the weave[52]
Then I struck her hip with a spigot
        Causing her, like flame, to leap
Thus drinks became available
        In gold and silver crockery
I said, when they resembled each other:
        Which one of them's the gold, really?[53]
They're the same; the only difference being
        One is solid; the other flows free
Some cups were smooth; others engraved
        With pictures of crucifixes and priests[54]
Reciting their Gospel, while above them's
        A sky of wine whose stars are beads[55]
As though they were pearls, scattered
        By the hands of virgins, playfully

NB: Philip Kennedy writes at some length about this poem in both A Genius of Poetry *and* The Wine Song. *Apart from its obvious autobiographical significance, it's among the most stylistically and thematically rich of the* khamriyyat; *appropriating and then overturning the classical poetic form and lexicon in a sophisticated device that asserts the superiority of Baghdad bohemianism over both piety and the pre-Islamic Bedouin mores, symbolised in the 'vanishing' like a desert trace of the mosque 'that combined* virtus *and religion'.*

To take just one example, where this pre-Islamic virtus *(Arabic* muruwwa*) demanded that a man give up the hedonistic indulgence of his youth once his hair began to grey – and Islam demanded he give it up in all cases – the poem instead describes its author's transformation from a boyhood of mosque-attending probity to an adulthood of hard drinking. As Kennedy puts it, 'The new order of religion (Islam) is placed alongside the old order inherent in the desert motifs; both are superseded by the celebration, in the putative present, of indulgence in wine' (*The Wine Song*, p. 112).*

On the autobiographical point, while the poet unambiguously refers in the seventh hemistich to male 'youths' (fitya*), it doesn't seem inconceivable that he might also have had his onetime female lover, Janan, in mind when describing the misfortunes that led to his move from Basra to Baghdad in the late 780s. Almost every detail of this section – the reference to companions 'scattered to the winds across countries'; their departure irreversible; Time never to 'beget others like them' – is consistent with the reports of Janan being sent away from Basra by her masters, prompting the heartbroken poet (who would never love a woman again) to relocate to the capital.*

A Will[56]

My dear friends, by God, don't dig
A grave for me but in Qutrabbul
Between the presses of the vineyards
Not among hyacinth bundles
Perhaps I shall hear, in my grave
The sound of feet on the presses rumble
And if I die on Syria's land
Don't leave me far from al-Furzul[57]

VII

'Pour for Us, for Today is Ram Day'

Miscellaneous mischief

The Doctor's Prescription[1]

I asked my brother Abu 'Isa
        Jibreel;[2] a man who's rational
I said, 'Wine amazes me'
        He said, 'Too much is lethal'
I said, 'Quantify it, then'
        He said – and his word's final:
'I've found that Man's natures
        'At root are quadruple[3]
'Therefore, four for every four;
        'Each nature gets a cupful
'Never exceed that number
        'For therein lies trouble'

NB: Al-Isfahani notes that the above poem was also attributed to Abu Nuwas' contemporary, al-Fadhl ibn 'Abd al-Samad al-Raqashi.

Anushirvan's Heritage[4]

We have a flock[5] whose young the wolf can't trap
Nor do the males' roars make them afraid
Their colours, when examined, tend toward
Reddish-black, although their fur is jade[6]
Were men to set out to milk them, they
Would find it was wine, not milk, they made
Her pastures are the Sarsar's[7] west banks
And Qutrabbul, Salihiyyah and 'Aqr's[8] shade
Heritage of Anushirvan,[9] not that
Left by Tameem or Bakr's[10] brigade
I spent my night with them, and a Lady's son
Of noble descent, though with funds mislaid

Ram Day[11]

Pour for us, for today is Ram Day[12]
A day superior to all others
Wine more blissful than the smile
Of the beloved to the lover
Not harsh or offputting to one's nature
As the ear's put off by loathsome chatter
But a decade's daughter, purified
Lighting up night if poured from the pitcher
In springtime fields, on which the rains
Bucketed early, in torrential showers
Thus embroidering the earth with all
Sorts of elegant blossoming flowers
There you see the group like crescents, drinking
From wine aged in a Khosrow's cellar
With calendulas, plucked from the ground[13]
Which they've placed upon their ears

Do You not See the Sun has Entered Aries?[14]

Do you not see the sun has entered Aries[15]
And Time's weight has risen, and levelled the measure[16]
And the bird has sung, after babbling
And the wine has reached its fullest splendour[17]
And the land's robed in its ornaments
As if it were, with plants, embroidered
Drink, then, to the novelty of Time, for the
Face of Time's in youthful flower
Of wine driving out worries, so you
Needn't fear reproach or censure
Karkh wine, rendering all that is long
In life short, spreading hopeful ardour
Playing the mirage's game in the glass
If its bubbles join together
He says, 'Pour it straight' if you dilute
For him holding a small tumbler
Give us two of its qualities
Beauty, richness; thus is it exemplar
So pour this man as much as he's capable
And give that one all that he can shoulder

Wine and War[18]

Take wine, for it has many names
Including 'Remedy' and 'Disease'
Water, if mixed, can improve it
And water can be its defeat[19]
Many have said, 'They had a battle
'News and tales of which are replete'[20]
I told him, 'You're an astonishing man
'Tardy in getting to life's good deeds[21]
'Drink, and spare us their news and tales
'The people will make amends if they please'

Our Commander's a Songstress[22]

Pouring for a war that I wage[23]
In a garden packed with wine-glass-fillers
Our swords are roses and narcissi
Our insults are the words of the singer
Our mangonels are instruments
And ʻouds, once tuned and ordered
Our projectiles are filled wine cups
Fired off by their pourer
Our commander's a songstress
With lush jasmine we salute her
This is the war that we declare
Which harms not, but brings pleasure

Knight of the Arabs[24]

O Bishr,[25] what do I want with swords and war
When I was made for pleasure and delight?
Place no confidence in me, for I'm
Spineless in the heat of battle and fight
Were I to spot the Kharijites approaching
I'd bridle my foal at the sight
I've no clue about shields and helmets
Nor guards to stay the enemy's smite
My sole concern, whomever the victor
Would be my route of escape and flight
Were it but revelry, and drinking
With floral-necklaced[26] girls all night
And sleeping beside one to sup from
You would find me then the Arabs' knight

Acknowledgments

Of all the friends who've had their patience tested with midnight medieval literature inquiries, well beyond the bounds of propriety, individual mention is due to Firas Talhouk, who really only has himself to blame, having introduced me in a Beirut bar to the opener of CEASE YOUR REPROACH in the first place; Nada Sleiman, who will one day perfect the French translation of the *khamriyyat*; and Ayman Mhanna, an oracle on any subject, but perhaps wine and Arabic above all. I could never have read Abu Nuwas, much less translated him, were it not for Asia Haidar, a courageous friend and peerless teacher who did me the unreturnable favour of unbolting the locked portals of the classical Arabic language. Without access to the inestimable treasures of the Orient-Institut Beirut and American University of Beirut libraries, I would have been without the bulk of the texts on which these translations and the accompanying research were based. To have handled the late Philip Hitti's personal copy of W.H. Ingrams' 1933 *Abu Nuwas in Life and in Legend*, as well as a first edition of 'Abd al-Rahman Sidqi's *Alhan al-Han* signed by the author in 1948 (both in the AUB library) was certainly not the least of the pleasures or privileges of writing this book. Emma Moghabghab, Christy Choueiri, and their editorial colleagues at AUB's *Rusted Radishes* magazine have my gratitude for publishing three earlier *khamriyyat* translations in the November 2015 issue of their fine publication. Similarly, my then-editor at *Now Lebanon*, Hanin Ghaddar, gave me free rein on at least one occasion to write about Abu Nuwas for what was otherwise a hard-headed politics journal. James Bloodworth generously took time out of his own voracious book-writing schedule to offer invaluable authorial wisdom to a debutant, as did Michael Weiss, a writer whose singular brilliance on the page is matched only by his benevolence off it.

New York University's Professor Philip Kennedy, who's been producing the gold standard of Abu Nuwas scholarship since I was producing my primary school homework, had the exceptional grace to set aside the trifling matters of his students, his research, and the Library of Arabic Literature project he heads to subject a complete draft of this manuscript to positively microscopic scrutiny. By not only rescuing me from numerous embarrassments and pointing me in the direction of edifying further reading, but even suggesting stylistic improvements in the wording of certain translations, to say he left me chastened with gratitude would be the least of it.

Michael Dwyer at Hurst Publishing has put me in his lifelong debt by agreeing to transform my private obsession of three years into the elegant volume you now hold in your hands. For their dedication, professionalism, and superlative taste in writers, I could not possibly salute him and his team enough.

Lavish praise is likewise due to Everitte Barbee for applying his exceptional talents to the creation, at very short notice and in record time, of the magnificent artwork found on this book's cover. For the flash of fecundity that led to its concept, credit is due John Tattarakis.

An *'usba* of additional comrades and *nudama'* too numerous to name, from Beirut to Dubai and beyond, have each contributed over the years to this endeavour in more ways than they know. I must commend my parents, John and Barbara, for their foresight in having me born in Jeddah and raising me in the United Arab Emirates, thereby making my eventual rendezvous with the *khamriyyat* inevitable from the outset. Their unyielding support, as well as that of my siblings, Emily and Josh, is and has ever been an indispensable source of sustenance. As for my wife, Mia, all authors are wont to say they couldn't possibly have produced their books without their spouses' backing, but in the present case there's nothing remotely trite or perfunctory about the statement. Mia didn't just nonchalantly throw together this book's dashing cover design; she provided palpable, practical assistance at every stage of its composition, as indeed she has throughout all of my professional writing years, such as they are. For her love, Abu Nuwas at the height of his powers could not have put into words my appreciation.

Notes

Introduction

1. From Hamza ibn al-Hasan al-Isfahani's introduction to his tenth-century collection of Abu Nuwas' poems, as cited in Wagner, Ewald, *Diwan Abi Nuwas al-Hasan ibn Hani' al-Hakami* ('The Collected Poems of Abu Nuwas al-Hasan ibn Hani' al-Hakami'), with Gregor Schoeler, Beirut, 2015, Book I, pp. 19–20.
2. Ingrams, William Harold, *Abu Nuwas in Life and in Legend*, privately published in Mauritius, 1933, p. ii.
3. It ought to go without saying that any attempt at biography for a figure who lived over 1,200 years ago is necessarily something of a fumble in the dark; a patchwork of a hodgepodge of source materials, almost all of them secondary, any one of which may be spurious, legendary, embellished, misattributed, or otherwise less than fully reliable for any number of reasons. Consider, for comparison's sake, that historians still know little with certainty about the early life of the Prophet Muhammad. What follows, then, is ultimately only a rough sketch of the picture as it has been portrayed in the surviving medieval accounts.
4. Medieval sources differ quite substantially as to his birth year, with claims ranging from 753 to 767. There is broad agreement, however, that he died shortly after the September 813 death of the Caliph al-Amin, whom he elegised, and that he did so at the age of fifty-nine in Islamic years, corresponding

to fifty-seven in Gregorian years. If we take 814 and 815 as his most likely death years, his corresponding birth years would be 757 or 758.

5. Sidqi, 'Abd al-Rahman, *Qissat Hayatihi wa Shi'rih* ('Abu Nuwas: The Story of his Life and Poetry'), Dar Ihya' al-Kutub al-'Arabiyya, 1944, p. 13. Much of the ensuing biographical information is based on Sidqi's work, which synthesises the major medieval accounts.
6. Sidqi, op. cit., p. 15.
7. From *zandaqa*, a Persian-origin word used in 'Abbasid times to describe those who professed Islam outwardly while secretly being Zoroastrians or Manicheans, later coming to mean an infidel more generally.
8. Al-'Aqqad, 'Abbas Mahmud, *Dirasa fi al-Tahleel al-Nafsani wal-Naqd al-Tareekhi* ('Abu Nuwas: A Study in Psychological Analysis and Historical Commentary'), Nahdet Misr, 2007, p. 79.
9. Literally 'The Departers', a violent splinter sect that rejected both the main contenders (Mu'awiya ibn Abi Sufyan and 'Ali ibn Abi Talib) in the leadership dispute that followed the murder of the third caliph, 'Uthman. They would go on to assassinate the then-Caliph 'Ali in Kufa in 661, and remained a threat to Umayyad and 'Abbasid caliphs for centuries. For their extensive practice of *takfir* (declaring opponents to be *kuffar*; 'disbelievers'), they have been likened in recent years to the jihadists of Al-Qa'ida and the Islamic State.
10. Literally the 'Followers' or 'Partisans' of 'Ali ibn Abi Talib, the Prophet's cousin and son-in-law, whose caliphate (656–61) was rejected by Mu'awiya ibn Abi Sufyan, the governor of Syria, who would found the Umayyad dynasty following 'Ali's murder by the Khawarij in 661. Generally opposed to the Umayyad, 'Abbasid, and Ottoman caliphates, the Shi'a today represent Islam's second-largest denomination.

11. That is, those who held that only descendants of ʿAli ibn Abi Talib were fit to rule the caliphate – a criterion which excluded the ʿAbbasids, who claimed descent instead from the Prophet's uncle, al-ʿAbbas ibn ʿAbd al-Muttalib.
12. Sidqi, op. cit., pp. 21–2.
13. Ibn Manthur, *Abu Nuwas: Fi Tareekhihi wa Shiʿrihi wa Mabadhilihi wa ʿAbathihi wa Mujoonih* ('Abu Nuwas: On His History, Poetry, Private Life, Levity, and Ribaldry'), edited by ʿUmar Abu al-Nasr, Matbaʿat al-Najwa, 1969, p. 21.
14. The non-Qur'anic anecdotal accounts, originally oral, later documented in writing, of what Muslims believe to be the sayings and doings of the Prophet Muhammad.
15. Sidqi, op. cit., p. 19.
16. Ibid.
17. Sidqi puts the year of his arrival in Kufa at 'around 156 AH', corresponding to 772–3 AD, i.e., when al-Hasan was between fourteen and sixteen (ibid., p. 35).
18. Ibid., p, 44.
19. Ibid., p. 32.
20. Kennedy, Philip F., *Abu Nuwas: A Genius of Poetry*, Oneworld Publications, 2005, p. 5.
21. Sidqi, op. cit., p. 73.
22. Ibid., p. 82.
23. I.e. tears.
24. Referring to the *latma*, a ceremonial beating of the chest performed by mourners.
25. Wagner, *Diwan*, Book IV, p. 15.
26. Wagner, *Diwan*, Book IV, pp. 42–3.
27. Al-Isfahani writes that al-Ahmar encouraged him to take a nickname inspired by one of the pre-Islamic Yemeni kings, and al-Hasan chose 'Dhu Nuwas' (d. c. 525) – 'He with the Dangling Sidelock' – presumably on account of his hairstyle (Wagner, *Diwan*, Book I, p. 12). Al-Suli also ascribes the name to the same Yemeni king (ibid., Book VI, pp. 3–4).

28. Sidqi, op. cit., pp. 93–4.
29. Quote and figures from Marozzi, Justin, *Baghdad: City of Peace, City of Blood*, Penguin, 2015, pp. 12–15, and Hitti, Philip K., *History of the Arabs: From the Earliest Times to the Present*, Revised tenth edition, Palgrave Macmillan, 2002, p. 293.
30. Hitti, op. cit., p. 293.
31. Ibid., p. 301.
32. Ibid., p. 300.
33. Ibid., p. 298.
34. Modern historians have called into question the true significance of this institution. 'Far from being a real university', writes Hugh Kennedy, it 'was basically a library [...] and the most important and original scholars of the period seem to have had no connection with it' (Kennedy, Hugh, *The Court of the Caliphs: When Baghdad Ruled the Muslim World*, Phoenix, 2004, p. 246). Kennedy writes in his notes that he bases this on Dimitri Gutas' *Greek Thought, Arabic Culture* (Routledge, 1998), adding 'it should be noted that [Gutas' conclusions] remain controversial'.
35. Hitti, op. cit., p. 315.
36. Ibid., p. 376.
37. Though, as the Encyclopaedia of Islam notes, 'The recent celebrity of the quatrains attributed to Khayyam is inversely proportional to the authenticity of many of them.' Fouchécourt, Ch. -H. De and Rosenfeld, B.A., "Umar Khayyam', in: *Encyclopaedia of Islam, Second Edition*, ed. by P. Bearman, Th. Bianquis, C.E. Bosworth, E. van Donzel and W.P. Heinrichs.
38 Ibid., p. 377.
39. English also, of course, derives 'algebra' from Arabic, as it does much else of its vocabulary, including but by no means limited to 'admiral', 'alchemy', 'alcohol', 'alcove', 'alkali', 'almanac', 'amalgam', 'assassin', 'average', 'coffee', 'cotton',

'crimson', 'elixir', 'ghoul', 'giraffe', 'jar', 'jumper', 'kohl', 'lute', 'magazine', 'mattress', 'lilac', 'nadir', 'orange', 'safari', 'saffron', 'sofa', 'spinach', 'sugar', 'syrup', 'sherbet', 'sorbet', 'talc', 'talisman', 'tariff', 'zenith', and 'zero'. Ptolemy's masterpiece is still known to this day by its Arabic name ('Almagest'), as are the vast majority of stars.

40. Ibid., p. 368.
41. Ibid., p. 306.
42. Sidqi, op. cit., p. 124.
43. Some sources (e.g., Ibn Manthur, op. cit., p. 194) go as far as to say the two had no contact whatsoever, though this seems impossible both intuitively and because Abu Nuwas' earliest biographer, Abu Hiffan al-Mihzami (d. 869), who knew the poet personally, recounts several anecdotes of their occasional meetings (Al-Mihzami, Abu Hiffan ibn Harb, *Akhbar Abi Nuwas: Al-Hasan ibn Hani* ['Stories of Abu Nuwas: Al-Hasan ibn Hani'], edited by Faraj al-Hiwar, Manshurat al-Jamal, 2011, pp. 101–4).
44. 'He would drink on two days of the week; Sunday and Tuesday', says the eleventh-century author al-Raqeeq al-Qayrawani (al-Qayrawani, Ibrahim ibn al-Qasim al-Raqeeq, *Al-Mukhtar min Qutb al-Suroor fi Awsaf al-Anbidha wal-Khumoor* ['A Selection from "The Variegated Pleasures of Descriptions of Wines and Strong Drinks"'], abridged by Nur al-Din 'Ali al-Mas'udi, edited by 'Abd al-Hafeeth Mansur, 'Abd al-Kareem ibn 'Abd Allah Establishment, 1976, pp. 210–1).
45. The utterance in question, according to Sidqi (op. cit., pp. 66–7), was in a poem, as follows: 'No man has ever come to us, after his death/ To say if he's in heaven or the fire'. (In Wagner's *Diwan*, the line is found in Book V, p. 225.) In his defence, Abu Nuwas is supposed to have pointed out that, whatever else might be said about the statement, it was undeniably *true*.

46. Wagner's *Diwan* contains five panegyrics for Harun (distinct from the elegies). More amusingly, one of the poet's ruder compositions, of a form replicated in around two dozen others, begins: 'Screw whomever you find among humans/ And forgive the sins of your brother [...] Accept the words of a scoundrel/ And defy al-Rashid when he orders' (Wagner, *Diwan*, Book V, p. 213).
47. In a lengthy poem addressed to al-Khaseeb, Abu Nuwas describes the route of his journey in detail, recounting how his camel convoy passed through sites including Palmyra, the Ghouta of Damascus, the Golan Heights, and Gaza (Wagner, *Diwan*, Book I, p. 244).
48. Al-Mihzami, op. cit., pp. 128–30. See O HANNA MONASTERY.
49. Sidqi, op. cit., p. 139. While al-Khaseeb seems on the whole to have been generous with money toward the poet, he could evidently be less so with wine on occasion. Abu Nuwas lampooned him for this in a poem that begins: 'Khaseeb withholds drink, and we hope/ For an offer from him – that'd be the day/Khaseeb isn't *khaseeb* [fertile] with his guest/ But rather barren land, desolate' (Wagner, *Diwan*, Book I, p. 407).
50. Encompassing parts of today's Iran, Turkmenistan, Uzbekistan, and Afghanistan.
51. See, e.g., Wagner, *Diwan*, Book I, p. 128.
52. Sidqi, op. cit., pp. 150–1.
53. Al-Mihzami, op. cit., p. 43.
54. 'From Greek-Latin *denarius*; the unit of gold currency in the caliphate, weighing about 4 grams' – Hitti, op. cit., p. 171. At the time of writing, 1,000 dinars of 24kt gold would be worth approximately £120,000.
55. Al-Mihzami, op. cit., pp. 139–40.
56. Sidqi, op. cit., p. 149.
57. Wagner, Ewald, 'Abū Nuwās', in: *Encyclopaedia of Islam*, Third edition, Edited by: Kate Fleet, Gudrun Krämer, Denis

Matringe, John Nawas, Everett Rowson. Consulted online on 23 March 2017: http://dx.doi.org/10.1163/1573-3912_ei3_SIM_0085

58. Cooperson, Michael, 'al-Amīn, Muḥammad', in: *Encyclopaedia of Islam*, Third edition, Edited by: Kate Fleet, Gudrun Krämer, Denis Matringe, John Nawas, Everett Rowson. Consulted online on 23 March 2017: http://dx.doi.org/10.1163/1573-3912_ei3_COM_22995
59. The question of which sibling initiated hostilities is still debated; see, e.g., Cooperson, Michael, *Al-Ma'mun*, Oneworld Publications, 2005, pp. 48–9.
60. See, e.g., Sidqi, op. cit., p. 161. It shouldn't be thought that al-Ma'mun was necessarily much more godly than his brother, for all his pretensions to being an *imam* (a quasi-divine Pope-like figure of utmost religious authority). Once caliph himself, al-Ma'mun too indulged a pronounced taste for the bottle and songstress. As we saw at the start of this introduction, he also personally had great esteem for Abu Nuwas – al-Qayrawani even quotes him rating the poet the best of all time (op. cit., pp. 235–6).
61. Kennedy, H., op. cit., p. 107.
62. War details based primarily on Kennedy, H., op. cit., as well as Kennedy, Hugh, *The Prophet and the Age of the Caliphates: The Islamic Near East from the Sixth to the Eleventh Century*, Second edition, Routledge, 2004.
63. Wagner, *Diwan*, Book I, pp. 342–3.
64. As P. Kennedy writes (*A Genius of Poetry*, pp. 26–7), less plausible alternative accounts claim, variously, that he was poisoned by the Nawbakhts; that he was beaten by the Nawbakhts; and, inevitably, that he 'died in a tavern drinking right up to his death'; an 'Abbasid Dylan Thomas sluicing to the end in a Baghdad White Horse Tavern.
65. Wagner, *Diwan*, Book I, p. 346.
66. Sidqi, op. cit., p. 189.

67. See Wagner, *Diwan*, Book I, p. 331, wherein a four-line panegyric is addressed to her.
68. See Wagner, *Diwan*, Book V, p. 99.
69. Kennedy, H., *The Court of the Caliphs*, p. 202.
70. Kennedy, H., *The Prophet and the Age of the Caliphates*, p. 153.
71. Ibid., op. cit., p. 145.
72. Kennedy, P., op. cit., p. viii.
73. Wagner, *Encyclopaedia of Islam*.
74. Ibn Manthur, op. cit., p. 64.
75. 'Abu Nuwas is for the modernists what Imru' al-Qays was for the ancients', said the Basran literary scholar Abu 'Ubayda (d. 824) (ibid., p. 48). Abu al-'Atahiya, for his part, is quoted as calling him the best poet of all time (ibid., pp. 55–6; and al-Mihzami, op. cit., pp. 151–3), while the ninth-century Syrian poet and author of the classic anthology *al-Hamasah*, Abu Tammam, said Abu Nuwas and Muslim ibn al-Walid were '[the pagan gods] al-Lat and al-'Uzza and I worship them both' (Ibn Manthur, op. cit., p. 49).
76. Ibn Manthur, op. cit., p. 256.
77. For an overview of the poet's oeuvre as a whole, P. Kennedy's *Abu Nuwas: A Genius of Poetry* and Ja'far Khuraybani's *Abu Nuwas: Al-Hasan ibn Hani'* are fine places to start.
78. Readers looking for a more rigorously academic analysis of the *khamriyyat*, and their roots in Umayyad, Rashidun, and pre-Islamic predecessors, are encouraged to consult P. Kennedy's *The Wine Song in Classical Arabic Poetry: Abu Nuwas and the Literary Tradition* (Oxford University Press, 1997). The 'Khamriyya' article in the second edition of the *Encyclopaedia of Islam*, written by the late Jamal Eddine Bencheikh, is also an excellent introduction.
79. Kueny, Kathryn, *The Rhetoric of Sobriety: Wine in Early Islam*, State University of New York Press, 2001, p. 36.
80. Usually these names contained information about the wines. *Mudam*, for example, is an aged wine, while *sulaf* is wine

made from unpressed, 'free-run' grape juice (*vin de goutte*). Both *kumayt* and *jiryal* are red wines, as opposed to the yellow *zarajon*; from Persian, meaning 'gold-coloured'. Other names, such as *diryaq*, betray Greek origin (*theriaca*, meaning 'antidote'). Al-Qayrawani provides a helpful guide to the meanings of over thirty-five words for wine found throughout Arabic literature (op. cit., pp. 28–39).

81. The oldest of the so-called *mu'allaqat* ('Suspended Odes') predating Islam; that of Imru' al-Qays (d. c. 565 AD), begins: 'Stop, let us weep in memory of a love, and a campsite'.
82. A watering site at which, in a battle in 609, pre-Islamic Arabian tribesmen defeated a Sassanid Persian force. Today a governorate in southeast Iraq bears its name.
83. A town on the Euphrates immediately west of modern day Fallujah, evidently known for wine in the poet's day. Destroyed by the Mongol invasion in the thirteenth century, its name survives today in the eponymous governorate in western Iraq. (It's striking how many places mentioned by the poet in connection with wine – Anbar, Tikrit, Fallujah, Heet, etc. – were until very recently ruled by the Islamic State group.)
84. A girdle worn by non-Muslims at the time to distinguish them from Muslims.
85. Al-'Aqqad, op. cit., pp. 103–4.
86. The pilgrimage to Mecca, incumbent on all capable Muslims at least once in their life.
87. Cayetano Ripoll, for instance, was hanged by the Spanish Inquisition for alleged deism in 1826.
88. The state was quite literally jihadist in other respects. Unprovoked military campaigns against the Byzantine infidels were an annual ritual, aimed at extorting spoils and, if possible, annexing territory. In 806, Harun – who personally participated in several of these raids – ordered the demolition of churches seized along the Byzantine frontier (Omar, F., 'Hārūn al-Ras<u>h</u>īd', in: *Encyclopaedia of Islam*, Second edition,

Edited by: P. Bearman, Th. Bianquis, C.E. Bosworth, E. van Donzel, W.P. Heinrichs. Consulted online on 23 March 2017: http://dx.doi.org/10.1163/1573-3912_islam_SIM_2747). Favourable assessments of the caliphate must similarly be tempered by the widespread practices of slavery, concubinage, eunuchry, and so on.

89. See, e.g., TELL US, WINE, HOW MANY YEARS HAVE YOU? and SEIZE THE NIGHT'S REMNANTS, AND BE DRUNK.
90. Qur'an 4:48.
91. Kennedy, P., *Abu Nuwas: A Genius of Poetry*, p. 7.
92. See, e.g., al-'Aqqad, op. cit., p. 139; Ibn Manthur, op. cit., pp. 245-6; Sidqi, op. cit., p. 165.
93. Wagner, *Diwan*, Book V, p. 14.
94. In fact, Twelver Shi'ism would not fully develop until the tenth and eleventh centuries, at the hands of 'such scholars as al-Kulaynī (d. 329/940–1) and above all al-Shaykh al-Mufīd (d. 413/1022) who produced the view of the imamate generally held by Twelvers down to the present day' (Kennedy, H., *The Prophet and the Age of the Caliphates*, pp. 225–6).
95. 'The creed of "Sunna and Community" so roundly condemned by al-Ma'mun now became [i.e. under al-Mutawakkil] the official position of the Abbasid state […] The creed of the [Hadith] literalists […] eventually developed into what is today called Sunni Islam' (Cooperson, *Al-Ma'mun*, pp. 124–5). As with Twelver Shi'ism, however (see previous note), Sunnism would not fully mature until the eleventh century, when the Caliph al-Qadir (d. 1031) formally denounced both Shi'ism and Mu'tazilism, and decreed veneration of the first four caliphs compulsory (effectively obliging the Shi'a to repudiate their view that only 'Ali and his progeny were entitled to the position). The breach between the two sects was now deeper and more explicit than ever: 'It was no longer possible to be simply a Muslim, one was either a Sunnī or a Shī'ī' (Kennedy, H., op. cit., pp. 239–40).

96. Dabiq, Issue 8, March 2015, pp. 39–56.
97. Wagner, *Diwan*, Book III, p. 324.
98. See, e.g., SPARE ME FROM KHURAFA'S SAYINGS. Elsewhere in the *Diwan*, he composes Hadith parodies, mimicking the format of the chain of oral transmission (*isnad*) and having his trusted authorities attest to the virtues of the libertine lifestyle. One of the less profane ones goes: 'We've narrated a Hadith/From Sa'eed, from Qatada/From al-Shu'bi – and al-Shu'bi/Is a sheikh of *jalada* [severity]/From Sa'eed ibn Jubayr/Saying Sa'd ibn 'Ubada/Said, "Whoever dies a lover/ Earns the prize of *shahada* [martyrdom; i.e., paradise]"'. Wagner, *Diwan*, Book V, p.238.
99. Ibid., Book V, p. 204.
100. Ibid., Book III, p. 4.
101. Hitti, op. cit., p. 359.
102. Kennedy, H., op. cit., p. 159.
103. A sixth-century king of the Sassanid Empire, the last Persian empire before the advent of Islam.
104. Tameem and Bakr are among the best-known of the north Arab tribes, hailing from the Najd desert, in today's Saudi Arabia.
105. Kennedy, P., op. cit., pp. 2–3.
106. Cooperson, *Al-Ma'mun*, p. 9.
107. See Wagner, *Diwan*, Book V, pp. 139–62.
108. The name of a friend of Abu Nuwas' who took up arms against the Khawarij, and tried to convince the poet to do the same (see Wagner, *Diwan*, Book V, p. 175).
109. Arabic *sukhub*; necklaces made from perfumed carnations.
110. There were 'Kharijite rebellions on a scale previously unknown in the province' following the appointment in 796 of an avaricious new governor, 'Ali ibn 'Isa ibn Mahan, writes Hugh Kennedy (op. cit., pp. 144–5). The year 794 had also seen 'the rebellion of Walid b. Tarif, a Khariji who was able to dominate much of the Jazira area [the territory north of Baghdad

between the Tigris and Euphrates] and prevent the government collecting any revenues' (op. cit., p. 141).

111. Wagner, *Diwan*, Book V, pp. 174–5.
112. 'Upon his Drinking a Bowl' (Wilmot, John, *Rochester: Selected Poems*, Oxford World's Classics, 2013, p. 33).
113. Amis, Kingsley, *Everyday Drinking: The Distilled Kingsley Amis*, Bloomsbury, 2009, p. 4.
114. 'There is nothing which has yet been contrived by man by which so much happiness is produced as by a good tavern or inn' (quoted in ibid., p. 37).
115. 'Ale, man, ale's the stuff to drink/ For fellows whom it hurts to think' ('A Shropshire Lad', poem LXII [Housman, A.E., *A Shropshire Lad and Other Poems*, Penguin Classics, 2010, p. 78]).
116. 'Wine cheers the sad, revives the old, inspires the young, makes weariness forget his toil, and fear her danger, opens a new world when this, the present, palls' (quoted in Amis, op. cit., p. 71).
117. 'Thou clears the head o' doited Lear/ Thou chears the heart o' drooping Care/ Thou strings the nerves o' Labor-fair/ At's weary toil/ Thou ev'n brightens dark Despair/ Wi' gloomy smile' ('Scotch Drink' [Burns, Robert, *A Choice of Burns's Poems and Songs*, Faber and Faber, 1966, pp. 104–5]).
118. Wagner, *Diwan*, Book III, p. 224.
119. See Kennedy, P., *The Wine Song in Classical Arabic Poetry*, esp. chapters 2 and 4.
120. Qur'an 2:219.
121. Qur'an 4:43. For the story about 'Abd al-Rahman ibn 'Awf see, e.g., the *tafseer* (exegesis) of Ibn Kathir regarding this verse.
122. Qur'an 5:90.
123. Wine differs from, e.g., pork consumption, which unlike wine is unequivocally and absolutely proscribed in the Qur'an by the use of the word *hurrimat* (Qur'an 5:3), of which *tahreem*

(literally 'to make *haram*') is the infinitive. In this respect, wine's status in Islam is closer to that of music than that of pork. Like music, wine receives its sternest rebuke not in the Qur'an but in the Hadith, which of course was not canonized in its final form until centuries after the Prophet's death (and Abu Nuwas'). It's surely telling that while both wine and music have been near ubiquitous features of Muslim societies throughout the ages, the same cannot be said of pork consumption.

124. Sidqi, *Alhan al-Han*, pp. 193–8.
125. The Saheeh Muslim collection quotes a Jabir ibn 'Abd Allah as saying: 'We were with the Messenger of God, May God's Blessing and Peace be Upon Him, and he asked to be poured [a drink], so a man said, "O Messenger of God, shall we pour you *nabeedh*?" and he said, "Yes", and [Jabir ibn 'Abd Allah] said the man walked away and brought a vessel with *nabeedh* inside', from which the Prophet then drank. (Saheeh Muslim, *Kitab al-Ashriba* ['The Book of Drinks'], *Fi shurb al-nabeedh wa takhmeer al-ina'* ['On drinking *nabeedh* and covering the vessel'].) See also the following from the *Encyclopaedia of Islam*: 'Several collections of traditions went so far as to mention *nabīdh* among the drinks prepared by Muḥammad's wives and drunk by him (Muslim, *Ashriba*, trads. 79–89; Aḥmad, i, 232–3, 240, 287, 320–1, 336, 355, 369, 372; ii, 35; iii, 304, 307, 313–14, 326, 379, 384, etc.). Abū Dāwūd (*Ashriba*, *bāb* 10) and Ibn Mādja (*Ashriba*, *bāb* 12) have preserved a tradition on this subject which is instructive. Ibn Mādja's version is given here: Ā'isha said "We used to prepare *nabīdh* for the Apostle of God in a skin; we took a handful of dates or a handful of raisins, cast it into the skin and poured water upon it. The *nabīdh* we prepared in this way in the morning was drunk by him in the evening; and when we prepared it in the evening he drank it the next morning". In another tradition of the same *bāb*, Ibn 'Abbās says that the Prophet

used to drink this *nabīdh* even on the third day; but what was left then was poured out.' (Wensinck, A.J. and Sadan, J., 'Khamr', in: *Encyclopaedia of Islam*, Second edition, Edited by: P. Bearman, Th. Bianquis, C.E. Bosworth, E. van Donzel, W.P. Heinrichs. Consulted online on 23 March 2017: http://dx.doi.org/10.1163/1573-3912_islam_COM_0490)

126. See Boutz, Jennifer Hill, 'Ḥassān Ibn Thābit, A True *Mukhaḍram*: A Study of the Ghassānid Odes of Ḥassān Ibn Thābit', Ph. D. dissertation, Georgetown University, 2009.
127. Al-'Askari, Abu Hilal al-Hasan ibn 'Abd Allah, *Diwan Abi Mihjan al-Thaqafi wa Sharhuh* ('The Collected Poems of Abu Mihjan al-Thaqafi and a Commentary Thereon'), Matba'at al-Azhar al-Baruniyya, 1900, pp. 17–18.
128. See HOW MANY A TAVERN-KEEPER I'VE FRIGHTENED and WE HAVE, IN THIS LIFE, HEAVEN'S WINE.
129. Al-Qayrawani, op. cit., p.161
130. For a detailed record of the Umayyad and 'Abbasid caliphs' drinking habits, see al-Qayrawani, op. cit., pp. 155–304.
131. Hitti, op. cit., p. 227. The late archaeologist Robert Hamilton believed he had located this pool at the eighth-century Khirbat al-Mafjar palace complex, just north of Jericho, which indeed features a pool in addition to a bath hall, and contains marble inscriptions to al-Walid's predecessor Hisham (whence its second name, Qasr Hisham, or 'Hisham's Palace'). As director of antiquities under Palestine's British Mandate, Hamilton was among the first excavators of the site. His contention regarding the pool has not been unanimously accepted, although, intriguingly, new excavations begun in 2012 have unearthed a previously-unknown 'large grape press' at the site (Whitcomb, Donald, and Taha, Hamdan, 'Khirbat al-Mafjar and Its Place in the Archaeological Heritage of Palestine', *Journal of Eastern Mediterranean Archaeology and Heritage Studies*, Vol. 1, No. 1 [2013], pp. 54–65).

132. Judd, Steven, 'Reinterpreting al-Walīd b. Yazīd', *Journal of the American Oriental Society*, Vol. 128, No. 3 (2008), p. 451. 'Even without his tent', writes Judd, 'al-Walīd managed to spend much of the pilgrimage in a stupor. Some reports even indicate that his inebriation forced him to rely on a servant to complete his ritual requirements in leading the observances'.
133. Osborne, Lawrence, *The Wet and the Dry: A Drinker's Journey*, Broadway Books, 2013, p. 184.
134. Bazmee Ansari, A.S., 'D̲j̲ahāngīr', in: *Encyclopaedia of Islam, Second Edition*, Edited by: P. Bearman, Th. Bianquis, C.E. Bosworth, E. van Donzel, W.P. Heinrichs. Consulted online on 10 July 2017: http://dx.doi.org/10.1163/1573-3912_islam_SIM_1929
135. Ahmed, Shahab, *What is Islam? The Importance of Being Islamic*, Princeton University Press, 2016, pp. 64–71. Jade wine vessels belonging to Jahangir still survive in the Brooklyn and Victoria and Albert Museums, inter alia, while several such coins are held by the British Museum.
136. Abu Zayd al-Balkhi (d. 934), for instance, wrote in his *Masalih al-Abdan wal-Anfus* ['The Welfare of Bodies and Souls'] that wine was 'the most beneficial' of all beverages; 'unique' in its provision of both bodily haleness and mental, even spiritual wellbeing (ibid., pp. 58–62). The same Abu Zayd 'also authored several works on the Qur'ān', adds Ahmed, and the Encyclopaedia of Islam states 'the works of al-Balk̲h̲ī on religious subjects were much praised by competent judges, especially his *Naẓm* al-*Ḳur'ān*, evidently a work of *tafsīr*' (Dunlop, D.M., 'al-Balk̲h̲ī', in: *Encyclopaedia of Islam, Second Edition*, Edited by: P. Bearman, Th. Bianquis, C.E. Bosworth, E. van Donzel, W.P. Heinrichs, Consulted online on 10 July 2017: http://dx.doi.org/10.1163/1573-3912_islam_SIM_1157). Ahmed notes further that Abu Zayd's approval of wine 'was shared by the physician-philosopher, Ibn Sīnā, who – when apparently not engaged in the problem of defining God –

routinely drank wine in good company.' See also, in this light, the poem THE DOCTOR'S PRESCRIPTION.

137. See Wagner, *Diwan*, Book V, pp. 248–53. One example: 'The envious have spoken about us/ Launching arrows and darts at us in flight/ Reproach and rebuke as much as you want/ "God spared the believers from the fight" [Quran 33:25]'. The line refers to the 627 Battle of the Trench, when the Muslims were besieged in Medina, and, according to the Qur'an, God sent a powerful wind to repel the enemies of the faith, thus 'sparing the believers' the need for further battle. The dry comparison of himself and his companions to the true believers (who, in Medina on that occasion, included the Prophet himself), and his censorious antagonists to the infidels, is, *mutatis mutandis*, a favourite motif of the poet's throughout the *Diwan*.
138. As quoted in Ahmed, op. cit., p. 159. For an extended critique of Hodgson's framework, questioning the very notion of distinguishing the 'religious' from the 'secular' or 'cultural' in Islamic literature, see ibid., pp. 157–75.
139. See esp. the so-called *khamriyya* of Ibn al-Farid (d. 1235).
140. Kennedy, P., *Abu Nuwas: A Genius of Poetry*, p. 136.
141. Wagner, *Encyclopaedia of Islam*.
142. Ingrams, op. cit., p. 48.
143. '*Al-Qahira tanfi ihraq diwan Abi Nuwas*' ('Cairo denies burning the collected poems of Abu Nuwas'), Al-Hayat, 14 Jan., 2001, https://goo.gl/qYMBCf, last accessed 28 March 2017.
144. 'Mystery surrounds Iraqi statue's missing glass of wine', Al-Monitor, 21 Aug., 2015, http://www.al-monitor.com/pulse/originals/2015/08/iraq-baghdad-monuments-memorials-sabotage-destruction.html, last accessed 28 March 2017.
145. '*Baghdad tu'eed al-hayat litimthal sha'iriha al-'Abbasi "Abu Nuwas"*' ('Baghdad restores life to the statue of her 'Abbasid poet "Abu Nuwas"'), Al-Arabiya, 15 July, 2015, https://goo.gl/KAVNda, last accessed 28 March 2017.

A Note on the Text and Translation

1. Wagner, *Encyclopaedia of Islam*.
2. From al-Suli's introduction to his recension, included in Wagner, *Diwan*, Book VI.
3. Specifically: Damascus' al-Thahiriyya Library (al-Suli); Istanbul's Ahmed Paşa (al-Suli), Beyazıt (Tuzun), Fatih (al-Isfahani), Köprülü (al-Isfahani and al-Suli), Ragib Paşa (al-Isfahani), and Süleymaniye (al-Isfahani and Tuzun) libraries; London's British Library (al-Isfahani and Tuzun) and former India Office Library (al-Isfahani); and Milan's Biblioteca Ambrosiana (al-Suli).
4. 'Atwi, 'Ali Najeeb, *Diwan Abi Nuwas: Al-Khamriyyat* ('The Collected Poems of Abu Nuwas: The Wine Odes'), Dar wa Maktabat al-Hilal, 2008.
5. From the foreword to his *The Book of the Thousand Nights and a Night* (1885).

POEMS

I

'What is Folly but Being Found Sober?'

1. Wagner, *Diwan*, Book III, p. 95.
2. Wagner, *Diwan*, Book III, p. 123.
3. Wagner, *Diwan*, Book III, pp. 99–100.
4. Wagner, *Diwan*, Book I, p. 55.
5. Wagner, *Diwan*, Book III, p. 222.
6. Specifically *sulaf*; wine made from unpressed, 'free-run' grape juice, known today as *vin de goutte*.
7. Wagner, *Diwan*, Book III, p. 223.
8. A polo-like game called *al-sawlajan* was popular at the time.
9. Wagner, *Diwan*, Book III, p. 93.
10. Wagner, *Diwan*, Book III, p. 167.
11. Meaning *nabeedh*, a weaker wine often made from dates, for which the poet frequently voices disdain (see, e.g., DISREGARD HIM WHO REBUKES IT; A CLERIC'S FATWA).

12. Wagner, *Diwan*, Book III, p. 181.
13. Babylon, founded in the third millennium BC on the eastern banks of the Euphrates, was one of the great cities of the ancient world, and at times the largest one on earth. It survived in various forms and under several empires until the death in 323 of Alexander the Great in its Palace of Nebuchadnezzar II, after which it fell into neglect (though it was briefly revived by the Sassanid Persians, to whom Abu Nuwas refers admiringly in other poems). Its name in the pre-Islamic monotheisms is synonymous with irreligious insubordination and profligate sin; usually involving intoxication: 'Babylon hath been a golden cup in the LORD'S hand, that made all the earth drunken: the nations have drunken of her wine; therefore the nations are mad' (Jeremiah 51:7). The New Testament describes a demonic 'great whore' of Babylon, 'with whom the kings of the earth have committed fornication, and the inhabitants of the earth have been made drunk with the wine of her fornication' (Revelations 17:1-2). It's possible that Abu Nuwas' notion of Babylon came from such Christian or Jewish sources, since the Qur'an mentions it only once, as a place of black magic (Qur'an 2:102). In any case, it seems natural that he'd have been drawn to its symbolism; that of earthly pleasures and impieties as opposed to the deprivations of pious probity.
14. Wagner, *Diwan*, Book III, p. 170.
15. There's a rather lewd double entendre here, for the word for 'male' (*dhakar*) can also mean 'penis'. The line can thus be read literally as: 'She grew angry when the penis touched her'.
16. Wagner, *Diwan*, Book III, p. 189.
17. Literally *jalees*; 'a sitter' at a social gathering.
18. He plays here on the near-homonymy of the Arabic words used for 'wine' (*rah*) and 'rest' (*raha*). According to al-Qayrawani (op. cit., p. 28), the two are actually etymologically linked; the wine being so named for the relaxation it brings its drinker.

19. Wagner, *Diwan*, Book III, p. 364.
20. The Arabic for 'spur disasters' (*tutheer al-dawahiya*) can also mean 'excite clever men'; the ambiguity may well be intentional.
21. Wager, *Diwan*, Book III, p. 205.
22. Wagner, *Diwan*, Book III, p. 85.
23. A favourite nickname of the poet's for wine.
24. That is, gives the sober man a hangover, and then (if drunk again) restores the hungover man to health.
25. Wagner, *Diwan*, Book III, pp. 88–9.
26. Literally meaning an 'elder', in the hierarchy of traditional Bedouin society the 'sheikh' was the head of the clan or tribe.
27. Wagner, *Diwan*, Book III, p. 97.
28. Wagner, *Diwan*, Book III, p. 122.
29. I.e., during pressing.
30. Wagner, *Diwan*, Book III, pp. 152–3.
31. Wagner, *Diwan*, Book III, p. 182.
32. Wagner, *Diwan*, Book III, pp. 171–2.
33. A proverb.
34. Wagner, *Diwan*, Book IV, pp. 212-3.
35. Arabic *nay*, sometimes rendered 'ney' in English. A woodwind instrument of Persian origin.
36. That is, of the 'oud.
37. That is, wine is being circulated among the drinkers so quickly that its scent trails behind the liquid itself, wafting in all directions.
38. Wagner, *Diwan*, Book III, p. 358.
39. That is, those sitting at a drinking gathering.
40. Wagner, *Diwan*, Book III, pp. 205–6.
41. Wagner, *Diwan*, Book III, p. 89.
42. Wagner, *Diwan*, Book III, p. 198.
43. Wagner, *Diwan*, Book III, p. 166.
44. The 'gold' being the wine's luminous glow, and the 'pearls' the bubbles created by its mixing with water.

45. That is, the stars Vega and Altair, known in Arabic as *Al-Nasr al-Waqi‘* (‘The Falling Eagle’) and *Al-Nasr al-Ta’ir* (‘The Flying Eagle’), whence the modern English names derive. They are the brightest stars in the Lyra and Aquila constellations, respectively; Vega is the second brightest star of the night sky altogether, when viewed from the northern hemisphere. One sees here another example of the poet’s interest in astronomy and science in general (c.f. DO YOU NOT SEE THE SUN HAS ENTERED ARIES; ANBAR WINE; and THE DOCTOR’S PRESCRIPTION).
46. Wagner, *Diwan*, Book III, pp. 106–8.
47. Stock names for female lovers in classical Arabic poetry, akin to the ‘Phyllis’ of Virgil and Horace (who was later borrowed for similar parodic purposes by, e.g., the medieval Latin satirists of the Carmina Burana, and, later still, Rochester and his contemporaries).
48. The first ‘wine’ is literal; the second, from her mouth, is the moistness of her kiss, often likened to wine (both in taste and intoxicating effect) in classical Arabic poetry.
49. A dirham (from Greek *drachma*) was ‘a thin silver coin slightly over 2 centimetres in diameter and weighing about 3 grams’ (Kennedy, H., *The Court of the Caliphs*, p. xxv). At current prices twenty thousand dirhams would be worth around £24,000.
50. Wagner, *Diwan*, Book III, p. 96.
51. Describing a wine as old enough to have been known to Noah is a running joke in the *khamriyyat* (see, e.g., SEIZE THE NIGHT’S REMNANTS, AND BE DRUNK; DEATH BY DRUNKENNESS). Though the Qur’an doesn’t include the story, in Genesis Noah is presented as the first man in history to cultivate wine and experience its transformative effects (‘And Noah began to be a husbandman, and he planted a vineyard: And he drank of the wine, and was drunken; and he was uncovered [i.e. naked] within his tent’ – Genesis 9:20-21).

It's possible that Abu Nuwas was aware of this via Jewish and/or Christian sources.

II

'Have an Early Drink, and Enjoy Yourself'

1. Wagner, *Diwan*, Book III, p. 16.
2. Or 'benefactions; favours; bounties'. Al-Isfahani notes in his commentary the allusion to Qur'an 7:69: 'Remember the blessings of God that you might prosper'.
3. Karkh is a Baghdad quarter on the west bank of the Tigris, still existent today, which in 'Abbasid times was an affluent commercial district southeast of the circular city walls built by the Caliph al-Mansur. It was also, evidently, renowned for its viniculture and nightlife (see, e.g., MAKE YOUR WAY TO AL-KARKH; HOW LOVELY IS A KARKH BAR; THE PLEASURES OF BAGHDAD). That Karkh long predated al-Mansur's Baghdad, being first founded in the fourth century by the Sassanid King Shapur II, may have added to its symbolic appeal for the poet.
4. That is, the drinkers, according to a note in the Köprülü Library (Istanbul) manuscript of al-Suli's recension: 'This is a metaphor; he means they are curing their hangovers by drinking it'.
5. Wagner, *Diwan*, Book I, pp. 65–6.
6. Wagner, *Diwan*, Book III, pp. 196–7.
7. Stock names, like the aforementioned Layla and Hind, for female lovers. Salma specifically was also the name of an actual woman in the love life of the Umayyad drinker-poet-caliph, al-Walid ibn Yazid (his wife's sister, no less). Almost all his amorous *ghazal* verse is addressed to her. One can only speculate as to whether Abu Nuwas, in saying, 'Put aside […] Salma, and drink', was humorously chiding his forebear.
8. An exhortation to gay sex. To ride the 'sea' was a euphemism for sleeping with women, as opposed to riding a 'mount' on dry land.
9. Wager, *Diwan*, Book III, pp. 120–1.

10. That is, the effaced 'traces' (*atlal*) in the desert sand of a former lover's campsite. This is another example of the poet ridiculing (as discussed in the introduction) the traditional topos of weeping at the *atlal*.
11. Arabic *muharaf*, a perpetually unlucky person; opposite of *mubarak*.
12. A canal between the Euphrates and Tigris, passing just south of the Round City.
13. More exactly 'and defy every old dimwit who is known to talk gibberish' (*wa-'asi kulla mufannadi*); i.e., the rebukers who say wine is forbidden, etc.
14. More precisely, money newly acquired (*tarif*) as well as its opposite, money inherited (*talid*).
15. Wagner, *Diwan*, Book III, pp. 245–6.
16. A former village in Iraq famed in the poet's day for its viniculture. In his *Mu'jam al-Buldan* ('Encyclopaedia of Countries'), the thirteenth-century author Yaqut al-Hamawi wrote of Qutrabbul that it was north of Baghdad, between the capital and the town of 'Ukbara, and 'the poets have mentioned it abundantly' in connection with wine.
17. The Arabic *kawa'ib*; 'women with full, round breasts'; appears in Qur'an 78:33, where they are listed among the rewards of paradise (along with a brimming wine cup, *ka'san dihaqan*, mentioned in the following verse).
18. There may be wordplay here, for the phrase 'witty discourse' (*turaf al-hadeeth*) can also be interpreted 'wonders of the Hadith', i.e., the purported sayings and actions of the Prophet, which make mention of heaven's full-breasted *kawa'ib* (see previous note).
19. Arabic *wa-lamma ajhali*; more exactly 'I did not behave with *jahl*', where *jahl* (lit. 'ignorance') is an undesirable character trait translated by James E. Montgomery as an 'uncouth lack of self-control' ('Abū Nuwās, The Justified Sinner?', *Oriens*, Vol. 39, No. 1 [2011], p. 98). P. Kennedy defines *jahl* more broadly

as 'the antonym of *ḥilm*, i.e. a lack of forbearance and therefore an inability to act or behave in accordance with the precepts of *muruwwa*', or manly virtue (*The Wine Song*, p. 282).

20. Wagner, *Diwan*, Book III, p. 256.
21. E.g., of a horse; a common expression tantamount to 'abandon restraint'. Compare A SAFEGUARD AGAINST THE CAPRICE OF TIME.
22. 'Ali Najeeb 'Atwi writes: 'He alludes by this to the soundness of their honours and the nobility of their morals' ('Atwi, *Diwan*, p. 303).
23. Philip Kennedy interprets this line carnally, noting a possible inspiration from the young Abu Nuwas' mentor, Waliba ibn al-Hubab: 'This one kisses this other one, and this one here kisses that other' (*A Genius of Poetry*, p. 64). One wonders whether there isn't also a profane allusion to Qur'an 3:103: 'Hold firmly to the rope of Allah all together and do not become divided'. Games of this kind with Scripture are by no means uncommon in Abu Nuwas (see, e.g., PRAISE THE BLESSINGS OF THIS WINE; A CLERIC'S FATWA; IF I SOUGHT PROBITY; THE HILLTOP TENT; O, DAUGHTER OF THE SHEIKH, POUR FOR US), while the mischievous equation of licentiousness with godliness in general is also a recurring motif (see, in addition to the above poems, CEASE YOUR REPROACH; I DRINK WINE; WE HAVE, IN THIS LIFE, HEAVEN'S WINE).
24. The opening line of the classic ode (*mu'allaqa*) of the pre-Islamic poet al-A'sha. Huraira (literally 'kitten') is the name of a woman. Abu Nuwas would have had more than just literary reasons for admiring al-A'sha: an esteemed wine poet, 'it is said' of him, writes Philip Kennedy, 'that he almost converted to Islam in 629 but fell just short of the act, dissuaded at the last minute upon finding out, already on route to visit Muhammad, about the Islamic proscription of wine' (*A Genius of Poetry*, p. 62).
25. Wagner, *Diwan*, Book III, pp. 174–5.

26. Perhaps meaning straight-up; undiluted (the poet elsewhere refers to mixing wine with water as 'marrying' it – see e.g. WATER'S WIFE and THE VINE COMES FROM BOUNTEOUSNESS). This would also explain the apparent strength of the wine alluded to in the sixth line. Alternatively, 'unmarried' may be meant in the sense of 'untouched'; compare DEATH BY DRUNKENNESS.
27. More precisely, with jet-black irises starkly contrasted with bright white sclerae – regarded as a feature of beauty.
28. Wagner, *Diwan*, Book III, pp. 191–2.
29. Strictly a gazelle fawn (*shadin*); alluding to a handsome youth.
30. The Quraysh are the tribe of north Arabian origin from which the Prophet Muhammad's family hailed. "Abbasi' refers to a descendant of the Prophet's uncle, al-ʿAbbas ibn ʿAbd al-Muttalib. The founders of the ʿAbbasid dynasty were so named because of their claim to be such descendants.
31. Ibn Mariya ('The son of Mariya') was the nickname of the pre-Islamic Ghassanid King al-Harith ibn Jabala (d. 569), whose mother was named Mariya.
32. Wagner, *Diwan*, Book III, pp. 282–3.
33. Sidqi suggests this line may be self-referential, given the poet was himself effectively orphaned since childhood (*Alhan al-Han*, p. 126). The allegory of wine as mother is also found in THE MOSQUE HAS VANISHED.
34. Wagner, *Diwan*, Book III, pp. 339–40.
35. Referring to mixing the wine with water, and the fizzing, frothing reaction that evidently was prone to occur when this was done.
36. A title of Persian kings.
37. Referring to the pictorial engravings on the vessel's outer surface. Compare THE ABANDONED TAVERN; HOW DID YOU GET TO MY HAREM. 'Perhaps the drawings here indicate the vessel was made in India', writes ʿAtwi (*Diwan*, p. 405).
38. An allusion to the fingertips' exceptional softness.

39. Wagner, *Diwan*, Book III, pp. 259–60.
40. The Kurdish homeland was then, as now, largely situated in the Zagros mountain range, where wine is known to have been made for millennia.
41. Wagner, *Diwan*, Book III, p. 221.
42. As in, God equalled the beauty of the full moon when He created this youth.
43. The opening line of a verse by the pre-Islamic poet Zuhayr ibn Abi Sulma, author of one of the classic *mu'allaqat* ('Suspended Odes'). Abu Nuwas often ended his *khamriyyat* with one of the characters drunkenly singing a line of older poetry, typically to musical accompaniment.
44. Wagner, *Diwan*, Book III, pp. 97–8.
45. That is, grey-haired.
46. That is, he wasn't literally dead, but unconscious.
47. Wagner, *Diwan*, Book III, pp. 354–5.
48. The Kharijites, or Khawarij, (literally 'Departers') were an ultra-fundamentalist splinter sect that, in the words of Hitti, 'caused rivers of blood to flow in the first three Moslem centuries' (op. cit., p. 247). The Khawarij rejected the legitimacy of both the main nominees to succeed the third caliph, 'Uthman (Mu'awiya I and 'Ali ibn Abi Talib), and would go on to assassinate 'Ali in Kufa in 661 with a poisoned sabre to the skull. The latter decade of Harun's reign saw considerable Kharijite violence in the province of Khorasan.
49. 'From Greek-Latin *denarius*; the unit of gold currency in the caliphate, weighing about 4 grams' (Hitti, op. cit., p. 171). At today's prices, a dinar of 24kt gold would be worth about £120.
50. Wagner, *Diwan*, Book III, p. 112.
51. Muhammad ibn Nasr al-Thaqafi, according to al-Isfahani.
52. Wagner, *Diwan*, Book III, pp. 139–40.
53. Referring to a large monastery on the Euphrates near al-Hira known as 'Umr Yunan, according to Sidqi (*Alhan al-Han*, p. 82).

54. I.e., the rising sun revealing the colours of the meadow's flowers.
55. A girdle worn by non-Muslims at the time to distinguish them from Muslims.
56. A place of Jewish religious study, as well as the venue for the festival of Purim (which is also *fuhr* in Arabic, from Hebrew via Nabatean *buhr*). Abu Nuwas would have had good reason to admire Purim, it being the occasion on which Jews are commanded in the Talmud to drink wine extravagantly.
57. It was evidently a common practice at the time to refer to wine in euphemistic or otherwise indirect terms; a practice the poet characteristically took pleasure in denouncing (see DON'T POUR IN SECRET).
58. In Islamic jurisprudence, the Arabic word used (*shubha*) refers specifically to ambiguity and indecision about the permissibility of something (i.e., it is neither clearly *halal* nor *haram*).
59. The Arabic word used (*tamweeh*) can mean both embellishment/distortion of the truth and the addition of water to something (such as a wine glass).
60. Grammatically, it is his 'doubting' that 'may covet betraying'. The intended meaning would seem to be: 'I shall stop doubting the virtue of you distorting the truth or adding water to my wine, lest it lead to us falling out'.
61. Wagner, *Diwan*, Book III, pp. 109–11.
62. That is, one of the effaced 'traces' (*atlal*) in the desert sand of a former lover's campsite (*rab*ʿ, in this case). This is another example of the poet ridiculing (as discussed in the introduction) the traditional topos of weeping at the *atlal*.
63. One of the oldest northern Arabian tribes, named after its founder, Asad ibn Khuzayma ibn Mudrika ibn Ilyas ibn Mudar ibn Nizar ibn Maʿd ibn ʿAdnan.
64. Tameem and Qays were the founding fathers of two of the oldest and best-known northern Arab tribes, known as the 'Sons of' Tameem and Qays, respectively. We see again here

the southern versus northern Arab rivalry with which the poet, affiliated with the southerners, played along (see also MANY A VINTNER I'VE COME TO, UNGUIDED; ANUSHIRVAN'S HERITAGE; A SAFEGUARD AGAINST THE CAPRICE OF TIME).

65. The Arabic word used (*al-a'areeb*) refers specifically to northern Arab tribes – see Philip Kennedy, *The Wine Song*, p. 38.
66. The *Moringa oleifera*, also called horseradish tree.
67. 'The Lion' was an ancient Arab solar mega-constellation, larger than and distinct from the Greek Leo. Its 'Nose' was an asterism comprising the stars Asellus Australis, Asellus Borealis, and the star cluster Praesepe. In the poet's time, the 'Lion's Nose' was prominently visible during the rainy season; the implication is that recent rainfall has turned the land verdant.
68. That is, money.
69. One can't help noting the moral parallel with Shakespeare's Lear: 'Why dost thou lash that whore? Strip thine own back; Thou hotly lust'st to use her in that kind For which thou whipp'st her' (Act 4, Scene 6).
70. Wagner, *Diwan*, Book III, pp. 193–4.
71. Awtas is a valley near Mecca where, according to Islamic tradition, Muhammad led a victory against pagan tribesmen in 630.
72. That is, unless it's out in the open, for all to see.

III
'Pour Me the *Haram* before the *Halal*'

1. Wagner, *Diwan*, Book V, p. 231.
2. An allusion to the wine of the Islamic heaven (see, e.g., Qur'an 47:15). See also THE WINE BARGAIN.
3. Wagner, *Diwan*, Book V, p. 230.
4. Alluding to wine being among the rewards of paradise (Qur'an 47:15). 'Avoid it' in this life, in other words, and it will be provided in the next.

5. This apparent declaration of abstinence is, of course, not sincere. Instead, it's a mock-exhortation to piety, not for its own sake, but for the eternal wine it will bring in the afterlife.
6. Wagner, Diwan, Book V, p. 209.
7. Arabic *'adhab*, a standard Qur'anic word (used over 280 times) for hell; i.e., polytheists will go to hell instead of Muslims. The word for 'protection' here, *wiqaya*, is also used multiple times in verb form in conjunction with *'adhab* in reference to protection from hell (e.g., Qur'an 2:201; 3:16; 3:191; 40:7). The poet is playing on his repeated assertion, in line with Murji'i doctrine (see introduction), that all sins will be forgiven on Judgment Day except polytheism (*shirk*).
8. Wagner, *Diwan*, Book III, pp. 345–6.
9. That is, the effaced 'traces' (*atlal*) in the desert sand of a former lover's campsite. This is another example of the poet ridiculing (as discussed in the introduction) the traditional topos of weeping at the *atlal*.
10. Wagner, *Diwan*, Book III, p. 169.
11. That is, the effaced 'traces' (*atlal*, or *diman* in this case) in the desert sand of a former lover's campsite. This is another example of the poet ridiculing (as discussed in the introduction) the traditional topos of weeping at the *atlal*.
12. He may be lampooning the great pre-Islamic master Imru' al-Qays specifically here; some of the Arabic wording (*dumoo'* and *'ala al-nahr*) calls to mind the ninth line of al-Qays' most famous ode.
13. That is, eighty lashes; the official punishment for alcohol consumption, determined by the Caliph 'Umar (d. 644), based on the Qur'an's mandating of the same for those who falsely accuse chaste women of adultery (Qur'an 24:4).
14. Wagner, *Diwan*, Book III, pp. 59–60.
15. 'Falluj' is almost certainly Fallujah, the city on the Euphrates 70km west of Baghdad, perhaps most famous (or infamous) in the twenty-first century as the site of the bloodiest battle

of the Iraq War between American-led Coalition forces and anti-Coalition militants. Yaqut al-Hamawi's thirteenth-century *Mu'jam al-Buldan* ('Encyclopaedia of Countries') contains no entry for a 'Falluj', but does mention 'Fallujah' as a town on the Euphrates. Modern-day Fallujah is believed to have been inhabited in one form or another since the Babylonian era. "Anat' is an alternative spelling of 'Ana, another Iraqi town of Babylonian vintage on the Euphrates still in existence today. 'The Arabs associated it with wine', writes al-Hamawi.

16. Al-'Uzza and al-Lat were two of three key goddesses worshipped in pre-Islamic Mecca (Manat being the third). The Prophet Muhammad vehemently opposed their worship, and their respective temples were destroyed on his orders in 630.
17. Luqman the Wise ('*Luqman al-Hakeem*') was a legendary sage revered in pre-Islamic Arabia, notably also mentioned favourably in the Qur'an, which names its thirty-first *sura* after him.
18. The word for 'insolent' here (*'ati*) carries specific connotations of rebellion against Allah. See, e.g., Qur'an 19:69 and 25:21. 'Heresy' comes from *zandaqa*, a Persian-origin word used in 'Abbasid times to describe those who professed Islam outwardly while secretly being Zoroastrians or Manicheans, and later coming to mean an infidel more generally. The charge of *zandaqa* was extremely serious – the poets Bashar ibn Burd and Salih ibn 'Abd al-Quddoos were both executed for it under the Caliph al-Mahdi (d. 785), and the Caliphs al-Mansur (d. 775) and al-Ma'mun (d. 833) were also notorious purgers of alleged *zindeeqs*.
19. Wagner, *Diwan*, Book V, pp. 222–3.
20. Yaqut al-Hamawi writes in his thirteenth-century *Mu'jam al-Buldan* ('Encyclopaedia of Countries') that al-Qufs was 'a famous village' slightly north of Baghdad, 'one of the heartlands of pleasure and centres of amusement and

gathering places of joy, producing fine wines and numerous taverns, frequently mentioned by the poets'. He then quotes another of Abu Nuwas' poems mentioning it.

21. Wagner, *Diwan*, Book III, p. 155.
22. Wagner, *Diwan*, Book V, p. 212.
23. Wagner, *Diwan*, Book II, p. 100.
24. Meaning Ramadan, the month of mandatory fasting.
25. The original Arabic in fact says simply 'killed', not 'crucified'.
26. The month that follows Ramadan.
27. Wagner, *Diwan*, Book III, p. 87.
28. 'Eid al-Fitr, literally 'the Festival of Fast-Breaking', is celebrated at the end of the month of Ramadan.
29. Wagner, *Diwan*, Book V, p. 220.
30. Wager, *Diwan*, Book III, pp. 164–5.
31. This line has at least three possible meanings, due to the ambiguity of the key verb, *mudarat*. Aside from the interpretation above, it could mean, 'We shall deceive He who is not deceived', i.e., God (which is how Sidqi understands it in *Alhan al-Han*, p. 121). A third possibility, which appears to be that favoured by Wagner, is, 'We shall conceal that which is not concealed'. I have opted for the above chiefly because it seems the most logical with respect to the preceding line.
32. Sidqi notes (*Alhan al-Han*, p. 144 n. 4) that the pre-Islamic poet al-A'sha had a line: 'I drank wine in al-Qaltayn, until/ I took a passing chicken for a donkey'. The phrase and variants thereof remain in use in Arabic today as allusions to advanced inebriety.
33. Wagner, *Diwan*, Book III, pp. 123–4.
34. Muhammad ibn Zuhayr, according to al-Isfahani. The same name is also mentioned in an anecdote pertaining to the poem GO TO HEAVEN.
35. The pilgrimage to Mecca, incumbent on every capable Muslim at least once in their life.
36. Places known at the time for viniculture and joie de vivre.

37. A town south of Baghdad, just off the pilgrimage route from Kufa to Mecca, known in the poet's day for wine and nightlife (see also WILL YOU TURN PIOUS AFTER THE HAJJ?). Al-Hamawi writes in his *Mu'jam al-Buldan* ('Encyclopaedia of Countries') that Tiyzanabad was 'one of the most pleasant outdoor sites, surrounded by orchards and trees and taverns and [grape] presses, and was one of the places sought out for pleasure-seeking and recreation'. The joke here is partly geographical; i.e., even if the poet managed to tear himself away from Baghdad and begin the pilgrimage, how would he restrain himself while passing Tiyzanabad? Indeed, one story has it that he encountered this problem quite literally on one occasion (see HOW DID YOU GET TO MY HAREM?).
38. Wagner, *Diwan*, Book III, pp. 124–5.
39. The poet plays here on the theological contradistinction between 'hope' [*raja'*] in divine forgiveness and 'fear' [*khawf*, or *khashya* in this case] of divine punishment (see SPARE ME FROM KHURAFA'S SAYINGS and, esp., GIVE BACK MY GLASS, for more on this). A marginal note in the Biblioteca Ambrosiana (Milan) manuscript of al-Suli's recension interprets this line to mean the poet hopes the Lord will make it so – i.e., that he will turn pious – but fears the attractions of Tiyzanabad will deny the possibility. A story recounted by Sidqi attributed to Sulayman ibn Nawbakht reveals (if true) an inside joke – see HOW DID YOU GET TO MY HAREM?
40. Places, like Tiyzanabad, known at the time for viniculture and joie de vivre.
41. Wagner, *Diwan*, Book III, p. 317.
42. Likely Sulayman ibn Abi Sahl ibn Nawbakht, of the Persian Nawbakht family who would be Abu Nuwas' longest-standing patrons in Baghdad.
43. The muezzin, or *mu'adhdhin*, is the one who recites the call to prayer (*adhaan*) at the mosque. See also HEAD TO THE MONKS' DWELLINGS.

44. Wagner, *Diwan*, Book V, p. 201.
45. Religiously prohibited and permitted, respectively.
46. Wagner, *Diwan*, Book III, p. 167.
47. *Tila'* was a name for wine that had been cooked until two thirds of its liquid had gone, making it religiously permissible in the eyes of some clerics (Al-Qayrawani, op. cit., p. 33).
48. I.e., Hell.
49. Wagner, *Diwan*, Book III, pp. 343–4.
50. Meaning *nabeedh*, a drink made from fermented raisins or dates, weaker in alcohol content than the powerful *khamr*, and deemed religiously permissible by certain clerics.
51. Wagner, *Diwan*, Book III, p. 240.
52. Religiously prohibited and permitted, respectively.
53. That is, the effaced 'traces' or 'remains' (*atlal*) in the desert sand of a former lover's campsite. This is another example of the poet ridiculing (as discussed in the introduction) the traditional topos of weeping at the *atlal*.
54. More literally 'That rids me of the *mabarik* of camels', where *mabarik* are designated camel-kneeling areas.
55. Wagner, *Diwan*, Book III, p. 345.
56. The word translated here as 'dim'; Arabic *safeeh*, more literally 'a fool', is found in the Qur'an in connection with disbelievers, i.e., those who foolishly choose to reject the true faith (see, e.g., Qur'an 2:13, 2:130). The pun thus insinuates it is in fact the poet's abstaining critic, not himself, who wants for piety (a trope seen also in I DRINK WINE; THE HILLTOP TENT; WE HAVE, IN THIS LIFE, HEAVEN'S WINE; WINE AND WAR).
57. Wagner, *Diwan*, Book III, p. 97.
58. Wagner, *Diwan*, Book III, p. 339.
59. Specifically, the two months of October and November (Arabic *tishreen*, of Syriac origin).
60. More literally 'her sash'.
61. Arabic *hawra'*; more precisely a woman with jet-black irises starkly contrasted with bright white sclerae – regarded as a mark of beauty.

62. Wagner, *Diwan*, Book III, p. 202.
63. Islamic eschatology holds that, on Judgment Day, a bridge (*al-sirat*) over hell will determine who is destined for paradise or the fire – the former making it safely across the bridge, and the latter tumbling into the flames.
64. Wagner, *Diwan*, Book III, pp. 119–20.
65. He plays here on the theological contradistinction between *khawf* ['fear' of divine punishment] and *raja'* ['hope' for divine reward, including forgiveness for sins] – see also WILL YOU TURN PIOUS AFTER THE HAJJ? and SPARE ME FROM KHURAFA'S SAYINGS. The second hemistich is more literally: 'And my hope [*raja'*] in Him is equal to my fear [*kheefa*, a variant of *khawf*] of Him'. In other words, the poet argues God's forgiveness obviates the need to fear Him. As discussed in the introduction, this ostensible belief in the near-totality of divine forgiveness – with its obvious implications for the permissibility of worldly transgressions – appears repeatedly in the *khamriyyat*, and has been interpreted by some as evidence of the poet's adoption of the doctrine of *irja'*.
66. Wagner, *Diwan*, Book III, pp. 209–10.
67. The Arabic word used is *qarqaf*, a wine named for the tremors it gives the drinker when hungover.
68. The Arabic word used is *munassaf*, referring either to a glass poured half-full, or to a form of cooked wine so named because the liquid was boiled until half of it evaporated (Sidqi, *Alhan al-Han*, p. 205). The poet had an intense aversion to cooked wine; cf. I DRINK WINE; O, DAUGHTER OF THE SHEIKH, POUR FOR US.
69. As Andras Hamori notes in connection with another Abu Nuwas poem, the word for 'winning' here, *faza*, is 'frequently used in the Koran in the sense of obtaining a place in Paradise' (Hamori, Andras, *On the Art of Medieval Arabic Literature*, Princeton University Press, 1974, p. 122). This typically

subversive borrowing from the Qur'an's nomenclature thus triggers several associations. Most obviously, it suggests one may drink and still reach heaven in the afterlife. It may also be an implied retort to Qur'an 3:185: 'He who is drawn away from the Fire and admitted to Paradise has attained [*faza*] [his desire]. And what is the life of this world except the enjoyment of delusion'. The 'winner', that's to say, is for Abu Nuwas not (or not only) he who drinks in paradise, but he who also drinks here in 'the life of this world' (cf. WE HAVE, IN THIS LIFE, HEAVEN'S WINE).

70. Wagner, *Diwan*, Book III, pp. 190–1.
71. 'Opinion' here (*ra'y*) is meant as a play on the Islamic jurisprudential term for a cleric's personal judgment on a theological matter; used in cases where alternative, preferred sources of law, e.g., the Qur'an, are insufficient. The following lines, therefore, form a kind of mock-fatwa decreed by the poet.
72. 'Ease' (*yusr*) and 'hardship' (*'usr*) appear together several times in the Qur'an. 'Allah shall bring about ease after hardship' comes in the financial sense in 65:7. The sentence, 'Verily, with hardship [comes] ease' is repeated in 94:5 and 94:6. 'Allah intends for you ease and does not intend for you hardship' (2:185) comes after decreeing exemption for travellers and the ill from fasting during Ramadan.
73. A line attributed to the 'Abbasid love poet al-'Abbas ibn al-Ahnaf (d. c. 808).
74. Wagner, *Diwan*, Book III, pp. 186–7.
75. This is a play on the Islamic jurisprudential concept of *qiyas* ('comparison' or 'analogy'), by which legislation in matters not explicitly covered in the Qur'an may be carried out by analogical induction. The poet is mocking his rebuker, who is evidently a theologian.
76. 'Greyness' (*shayb*) was often contrasted in pre-Islamic Arabic poetry with the 'youthful passion' (*siba*) of the first line. The idea was that men should put aside *siba* (and, by extension,

wine drinking) once their hair turned grey; a suggestion firmly rejected by the poet here.

77. That is, those seated at the drinking gathering.
78. Wagner, *Diwan*, Book III, pp. 222–3.
79. The Arabic word used for 'innovation' is *bid'a*, an Islamic jurisprudential term for a novel doctrine deemed heretical. The mischievous insinuation is that it is abstinence from wine, not its consumption, that is impious.
80. A reference to the wine of paradise, mentioned in, e.g., Qur'an 47:15.
81. The word translated here as 'libation', *raheeq*, is among the Qur'an's synonyms for the wine in heaven (see 83:25), though it has also meant superlative wine generally since pre-Islamic times (see, e.g., the *mu'allaqa* of Imru' al-Qays).
82. Abu Nuwas often ended his *khamriyyat* with one of the characters drunkenly singing a line of older poetry, typically to musical accompaniment. The line in question here is by the hard-drinking poet Abu Mihjan al-Thaqafi, a Companion (*Sahabi*) of the Prophet and thus among the very first Islamic bards to laud wine.
83. Wagner, *Diwan*, Book III, pp. 292–3.
84. Arabic *jam*; a 'wide vessel with short sides' according to al-Qayrawani (op. cit., p. 39). Several dictionaries (e.g. *al-Ra'id*; *al-Mu'jam al-Waseet*) describe the *jam* as being typically made of silver.
85. Monotheistic tradition holds that the descendants of Ham, a son of Noah, populated Africa. The implication is that the man is black; Sidqi writes that the sheepskin used to make drinking pouches was black (*Alhan al-Han*, p. 213).
86. More literally, 'That thins the dense weave of my Islam'. Meant either in the sense of alleviating piety's discomfort, allowing for relaxation, etc.; or weakening the robustness of his otherwise intact piety, and allowing sin to seep through the cracks.

87. The Arabic letter *lam*, corresponding to the English 'L', is shaped with a sweeping curve at the bottom: ل.
88. Meaning his ancestors more generally; a possible reference to his Persian (and therefore Zoroastrian) roots.
89. Wagner, *Diwan*, Book III, pp. 316–7.
90. Literally meaning 'an elder', in the hierarchy of traditional Bedouin society the 'sheikh' was the head of the clan or tribe.
91. More literally 'What is it you're waiting for?'
92. 'Cooked date wine', according to 'Atwi (*Diwan*, p. 375), 'which was religiously permissible (*halal*) for the Iraqis and was thus named "the Beverage of the Virtuous (*sharab al-saliheen*)"'. The poet had an intense aversion to such cooked wines; cf. I DRINK WINE.
93. That is, a religion.
94. 'Time' here carries the additional connotation of 'Fate', while 'the Hour' refers to Judgment Day. As Philip Kennedy explains (*The Wine Song*, pp. 144–7), the line mocks a trope then common in pious poetry (*zuhdiyyat*) whereby the attainment of middle age and the approach of death (and, with it, divine judgment) are held to be grounds for abstinence and repentance from the sins of youth.
95. Philip Kennedy calls this closing line 'an agnostic credo' (ibid., p. 147). The entire poem is richly imbued with ironic allusions to Islam. In the Arabic, the sixth hemistich ('And be not, of this, dubious') borrows the phrasing of the Qur'anic concept of *'ilm yaqeen* ('certain knowledge'). The word *sa'ileena* also has Qur'anic echoes (see e.g. Sura 12:7), and indeed the entire rhyme scheme, ending in the syllables *ee-na*, adopts 'the dominant assonance of the Qur'an', Kennedy writes. The professor also argues persuasively that the poem pays tribute in several respects to the pre-Islamic ode (*mu'allaqa*) of 'Amr ibn Kulthum.
96. Wagner, *Diwan*, Book III, pp. 286–7.

97. While this may be taken in a broader sense, he likely also alludes specifically to 'recovery' from the hangover (c.f. CEASE YOUR REPROACH; MY SOUL'S SISTER).
98. Religiously permissible.
99. The words vine (*karm*) and generosity (*karam*) are almost identical, and he seems to suggest here, perhaps not entirely facetiously, that they are etymologically related. In several other poems he associates drink with munificence, and, conversely, abstinence with meanness (c.f. YOUR REPROACH COMES FROM ENVY; SAY TO THE BEAUTY IN THE BLACK VEIL; POURING FOR BAGHDAD, AND THE DAYS; THE HILLTOP TENT; WHAT A WEAPON WINE IS; O, DAUGHTER OF THE SHEIKH, POUR FOR US).
100. 'Alluding' by the image of soiled leather, says 'Atwi, 'to unpleasantness of character and meanness of disposition' (*Diwan*, p. 345). See also DEFY THOSE, IGNORANT OF LOVE, WHO BERATE.
101. More literally 'tracing his ancestry through aged wine to the drinks partner [*nadeem*]'.
102. Wagner, *Diwan*, Book III, pp. 291–2.
103. The Arabic word used, *imam*, can mean both a common mosque prayer-leader and a far more senior, indeed supreme, religious authority; it was among the titles taken by caliphs. It's possible that the line is a dig at al-Ma'mun, who, when vying for al-Amin's throne (and condemning the latter's friendship with Abu Nuwas), declared himself to be the sole true *imam* of the age. However, it could equally be a playful jab at al-Amin, who, as we have seen, occasionally compelled Abu Nuwas to stop drinking, and to whom the poet elsewhere refers as the *imam* (cf. WAKE YOUR DRINKS PARTNER; I DON'T TASTE THE WINE EXCEPT BY NOSE; I'M FREED OF THE IMAM'S REPROACH).
104. Religiously forbidden and permitted, respectively. The poet refers either to grapes being *halal*, or to wine itself being *halal* in the very first years of Islam (see introduction).

105. A reference to the so-called *ghulamiyyat* trend that emerged during al-Amin's reign; namely, female slaves at parties dressed and groomed to look like males (cf. CEASE YOUR REPROACH; DON'T POUR IN SECRET).
106. Two Arabic letters, corresponding to English 'D' and 'L', respectively. When combined in Arabic they spell the word *dall*, meaning 'flirtation' or 'coquetry'. The line can thus be interpreted 'You've conquered my heart by your flirtation with me'. Alternatively, given the poet's predilection for using the shapes of letters to illustrate images (cf. A FRIEND OF MOSES), he may be alluding to the woman's curvaceous figure: the letters in Arabic are د and ل, respectively.
107. Wagner, *Diwan*, Book III, pp. 178–9.
108. The specific word used is *zeer*, meaning the highest-pitched string of an instrument, in this case a *tanbur* (see note 4).
109. More precisely, with jet-black irises starkly contrasted with bright white sclerae – regarded as a feature of beauty.
110. A long-necked stringed instrument found in Mesopotamia since the Akkadian era (third millennium BC).
111. The *takbeer* is the declaration '*Allahu akbar*' ('God is greatest'). It is a fundamental component of Muslim prayer, without which the prayer is incomplete and invalid. Perhaps the poet means here the group was too drunk by dawn to be capable of saying the words – in other poems, e.g. THE FINEST COMPANY A DRINKER COULD KEEP AND WINE and THE YOUTH, he describes such an affliction. Alternatively, he may mean they passed out, and thus resembled people praying in prostration, but were in fact unconscious.
112. Wagner, *Diwan*, Book III, pp. 223–5.
113. The Arabic verb *haddatha* means both to tell stories and to recount Hadiths (the purported sayings and doings of the Prophet Muhammad). There is thus an ironic double meaning: the line can be both 'That whomever meets dawn tells, about you, stories' and 'That whomever meets dawn narrates Hadiths quoting you'.

114. As in other poems, idolatry or polytheism (Arabic *shirk*) is the one sin to which the poet never admits. This is consistent with his stated belief in divine forgiveness (*ghufran*) – the Qur'an states plainly that those who engage in *shirk* will not be offered *ghufran* (4:48).
115. Wagner, *Diwan*, Book V, pp. 215–6.
116. The distinction made at the time between 'weak wine' (*nabeedh*) and the stronger potation (*khamr*, or in this case *'uqar*) has been discussed in the introduction. The joke here, which sets the tone for the rest of the poem, is that this 'learned cleric' affirms the religious rectitude of Abu Nuwas' preferred indulgences.
117. An oboe-like wind instrument.
118. The Qur'an specifically forbids prayer while intoxicated (4:43).
119. *Zakat* is a religious duty obliging Muslims to give away a portion of their income; one of the five mandatory so-called 'pillars' of the faith.
120. More literally: 'Even if Mecca were at [your] front door'
121. Likely a swipe at the Khawarij, one of whose tenets was that tyrannical rulers had to be opposed violently. The Murji'a, by contrast, whose doctrines Abu Nuwas occasionally appears to espouse (see introduction), were generally quietists opposed to the use of violence.
122. A carnal allusion: 'Take revenge' on tyrants by bedding their sons and daughters.
123. The significance of this line comes from Qur'an 4:58: 'Verily Allah commands you to return deposits to whom they are due'. The Arabic word rendered above as 'date debris' is *qitmeer*; literally a wafer-thin flake of husk between the seed and flesh of a date. Its use in the sense of something worthless is found in the Qur'an 35:13: 'And those you invoke other than [God] do not have power over so much as a *qitmeer*'.
124. Wagner, *Diwan*, Book III, pp. 2–4.

125. This opener is Abu Nuwas' most famous line, and one of the most celebrated in all Arabic poetry. Al-Isfahani cites a few antecedents in older verse, including the Umayyad poet Sabiq al-Barbari's 'Obstinacy in rebuke is, for him, temptation' and the pre-Islamic al-A'sha's 'Many a glass I've drunk for pleasure, and many others I've used as cures to recover'. The literary critic Muhalhil ibn Yamout ibn al-Muzarra' al-Sha'mi, in his letter to al-Isfahani included in the *Diwan*, also accredits to Ibn Udhaina the line, 'And my rebuker, by his rebuke, tempts me'. Kennedy further suggests a line by the Rashidun and Umayyad poet Haritha ibn Badr ('So rebuke me, for rebuke [of wine] increases my/ Desire for it, verily censure can tempt') as an inspiration (*The Wine Song*, p. 188). One could also note the Umayyad Caliph al-Walid ibn Yazid's 'Desist, O critics, from reproaching me/ Verily, rebuking me increases my wrongdoing' (Gabrieli, Francesco, *Diwan al-Walid ibn Yazid al-Umawi* ['The Collected Poems of al-Walid ibn Yazid the Umayyad'], Dar al-Kitab al-Jadeed [Beirut], 1967, p. 74).

126. As mentioned in the introduction, during the Caliph al-Amin's reign there came to be a phenomenon at court known as the *ghulamiyyat*; that is, female slave-servants dressed and groomed to look like young men.

127. 'Time' (*zaman*) is meant here in the Shakespearean sense of 'fate', 'fortune', or 'destiny' – the 'vicissitudes of Time' were the predominant cosmic force of pre-Islamic Arabia; the perennial bane of the *Jahili* poet. In their Dionysian resplendence, these youths have managed almost preternaturally to tame this almighty caprice; to blunt Time's scythe, nullifying its power to 'afflict' them with anything other than what they desire. The Arabic *fama yuseebuhum illa bima sha'u* also has echoes of the Qur'an's *yuseebu bihi man yasha'u* ('[Allah] strikes with [good or bad] whomever He wills'), found in 10:107; 13:13; and 24:43.

128. More stock names for female lovers.

129. Durra (literally 'pearl') was the name of 'the servant-girl of Abu Nuwas', according to Kennedy (*A Genius of Poetry*, p. 68). A marginal note in the Biblioteca Ambrosiana (Milan) manuscript of al-Suli's recension says simply that she was 'a woman'. Mention is made elsewhere in the *Diwan* of a slave named Durra who was in love with the poet (Book I, p. 92).
130. The poet channels here one of the tenets of a then-current Islamic doctrine known as *irja'* (lit. 'postponement'), discussed in the introduction. The final two lines are, in fact, a lampoon of one Ibrahim al-Natham, a leading cleric of a rival school, the Mu'tazila, who held wine drinking to be an unpardonable sin, and is said to have confronted his former friend Abu Nuwas about the matter in person. Overall, though relatively short, the poem is arguably the poet's magnum opus; coursing swiftly but seamlessly through his signature themes in a rousing defence of the fierce individualism of which he may still be Arabic literature's most eloquent voice.

IV

'How Many a Tavern-Keeper I've Frightened...'

1. Wagner, *Diwan*, Book III, pp. 92–3.
2. The opening line of another of his poems, O HANNA MONASTERY. The 'Hanna Monastery' (*Dayr Hanna*) is mentioned in Yaqut al-Hamawi's thirteenth-century *Mu'jam al-Buldan* ('Encyclopaedia of Countries') as being on the outskirts of Kufa and al-Hira, possibly the same (al-Hamawi says 'I don't know') as an old one of the same name in al-Hira dating back to the pre-Islamic Lakhmid kingdom, which ruled the Christian city from the third century till the start of the seventh. The hard-drinking Umayyad Caliph al-Walid ibn Yazid (d. 744) is said to have once made the journey from Damascus to the Hanna Monastery expressly for the purpose of sampling its legendary wine (Sidqi, *Alhan al-Han*, p. 48).

Abu Nuwas refers elsewhere to his general fondness for al-Hira and its viniculture (see e.g. I MISS AL-HIRA; HEAD TO THE MONKS' DWELLINGS).

3. Wagner, *Diwan*, Book I, pp. 333–4.
4. A more literal translation of the same line appearing at the end of A SCENT OF MUSK. The Arabic phrasing of 'where the monks dwell' recurs also in HEAD TO THE MONKS' DWELLINGS, which bears other resemblances to this poem.
5. The word 'recover' here (from the Arabic root *sahw*) is also used in the sense of sobering up.
6. That is, attractive youths.
7. A reference to their asceticism. Compare, from HEAD TO THE MONKS' DWELLINGS: 'Make for a group whose members have turned/ Frail as ghosts from worshipping'.
8. Meaning hair partings, i.e., monks.
9. Wagner, *Diwan*, Book III, pp. 91–2.
10. The word used for 'monks' dwellings' (*ukayrah*) is the same as that used in connection with the 'Hanna Monastery' in A SCENT OF MUSK and O HANNA MONASTERY, which in turn is placed by Yaqut al-Hamawi on the outskirts of al-Hira. The poem I MISS AL-HIRA also bears resemblances to this one.
11. The 'sound you loathe' being the mosque's call to prayer, and the 'peasant' being the muezzin. This is a pun, for the Arabic 'peasant' (*fallah*) is almost identical to 'success' (*falah*), a word used in the daily call to prayer (*Hayya 'ala al-falah* – 'Come to success'). See also HAND ME A GLASS TO DISTRACT.
12. Wagner, *Diwan*, Book V, p. 161.
13. Al-Hira was an ancient city south of Kufa in Iraq founded c. 200 AD by Yemeni tribespeople. It became the capital of the pre-Islamic Arab Lakhmid kingdom, a prosperous and strategic midpoint between the Byzantine Empire on the one hand and Sassanid Persia on the other. Much of the local population was Nestorian Christian and one Lakhmid king, al-Nu'man III, converted from paganism to the faith. The city

fell to the Muslim army of Khalid ibn al-Walid in 633, and while it continued to exist for a few centuries, today 'where al-Ḥīrah once stood lie a few low mounds', wrote the late Philip Hitti (op. cit., p. 84 n. 3). It holds an eminent place in the history of Arabic literature, including wine poetry: 'The Christian poet 'Adi b. Zayd (d. c. 600) from Hira is supposed to have been the first poet to compose a large number of [...] independent *khamriyyat*', writes Philip Kennedy (*The Wine Song*, p. 6). Abu Nuwas also expresses his fondness for al-Hira in other poems – see, e.g., A SCENT OF MUSK; HEAD TO THE MONKS' DWELLINGS.

14. Arabic *yawm al-nahr*, an alternative name for 'Eid al-Adha; 'the Festival of the Sacrifice', suggesting the poet would spend this holiest of Muslim holidays drinking in al-Hira.
15. Wagner, *Diwan*, Book III, p. 168.
16. A watering site at which, in a battle in 609, pre-Islamic Arabian tribesmen defeated a Sassanid Persian force. Today a governorate in southeast Iraq bears its name.
17. A town on the Euphrates in what is today western Iraq, evidently known for wine in the poet's day. Founded several centuries before Islam immediately west of today's Fallujah, al-Anbar was originally a Sassanid Persian town, later destroyed by the Roman emperor Julian in 363. Once rebuilt, it became a cosmopolitan centre, home to pre-Islamic Lakhmid Arabs, Jews, and Assyrian Christians, among others. The first 'Abbasid caliph, Abu al-'Abbas al-Saffah, made al-Anbar capital of the empire, a distinction it enjoyed until his successor al-Mansur built Baghdad. Though al-Anbar was eventually destroyed by the Mongols, it gives its name today to the large Anbar Governorate, which saw some of the fiercest fighting between American forces and al-Qa'ida militants after the 2003 invasion. Almost all of its populated areas are now, or were until very recently, ruled by the Islamic State group.

18. 'Young gazelle' refers to a handsome youth.
19. More stock women's names. An Umm 'Amr, for example, is mentioned in the famous pre-Islamic ode of 'Amr ibn Kulthum, while an Umm Najiya appears in the work of the Umayyad poet Jarir.
20. Wagner, *Diwan*, Book III, p. 199.
21. Susa was one of the oldest and grandest cities of the ancient world, located in what is today the Ahvaz region of Iran. Capital city of the pre-Iranic Elamite state, it was also later at times the capital of the Persian Empire.
22. The name, not necessarily fictitious, of the seemingly Persian proprietor of this Karkh tavern.
23. That is, non-Muslim. Given his likely Persian identity, 'Qadoos' is probably a Zoroastrian.
24. A *kurta* is a collarless shirt of Persian or Indian origin. Khorasan was a historical province spanning parts of today's Iran, Turkmenistan, Uzbekistan, and Afghanistan.
25. Two prominent cities in Khorasan, today located in Turkmenistan and Iran, respectively. Merv, the capital of the province, was where the black flags of the 'Abbasid rebellion against the Umayyads were first raised, in 747.
26. Wagner, *Diwan*, Book III, p. 319.
27. Dark robes associated with Persians.
28. The Banu Tameem ('Sons of Tameem') are among the most famous of northern Arab tribes, hailing originally from the Najd desert in today's Saudi Arabia.
29. Specifically, Abu Nuwas' father was affiliated with the Hakam tribe. We see once again here the rivalry between northern and southern tribal confederations with which the poet played along (see also YOUR REPROACH COMES FROM ENVY; ANUSHIRVAN'S HERITAGE; A SAFEGUARD AGAINST THE CAPRICE OF TIME).
30. That is, quantity-wise, due to evaporation.
31. Wagner, *Diwan*, Book III, pp. 183–6.

32. Sabat was a place near al-Mada'in (the Arabic name for Ctesiphon, former capital of the pre-Islamic Persian Sassanid Empire, on the Tigris around 35km southeast of Baghdad). Al-Isfahani records the Nawbakhts as saying Abu Nuwas was travelling to al-Mada'in with some of their relatives when the group came upon the ruins of a gathering place in Sabat, about which the poet composed this verse.
33. Wagner, *Diwan*, Book III, pp. 258–9.
34. A metaphor for a handsome youth.
35. The poet often uses pearls as a metaphor for bubbles in wine.
36. Wagner, *Diwan*, Book III, pp. 137–8.
37. Wagner, *Diwan*, Book III, pp. 237–9.
38. A note in the Köprülü Library (Istanbul) manuscript of al-Suli's recension reads: 'That is, the dogs have become familiar with those who come at night, so they don't bark at them'. Compare CRACKS IN THE HEAVENS.
39. That is, the poet sees alcoholic and non-alcoholic drinks as equally permissible (*muhallal*) from the religious standpoint.
40. Referring to the preparation of the weaker *nabeedh* drink by hand, in contrast to the stronger *khamr*, pressed by foot.
41. More literally 'if it withholds [greedily] or does not withhold'; perhaps an amorous compliment to the pourer, whose palm would be lovely even if it weren't supplying wine.
42. Meaning the seventh-century poet Hassan ibn Thabit, a Companion (*Sahabi*) of the Prophet Muhammad often described as his 'court poet' or 'poet laureate'.
43. More literally 'Was killed, damn you, so give me one that hasn't been killed'. The line is from a poem by Hassan ibn Thabit (see previous note) that features extensive descriptions of wine drinking. According to the late 'Abd al-Rahman al-Barquqi, who wrote a book-length commentary on the poems of Hassan, by 'killed' he means the wine has been mixed with water. 'Give me one that hasn't been killed' thus means 'give me one straight up' (Al-Barquqi, 'Abd al-Rahman,

Sharh Diwan Hassan ibn Thabit al-Ansari ['A Commentary on the Collected Poems of Hassan ibn Thabit al-Ansari'], Al-Matba'a al-Rahmaniyya, 1929, p. 311). Abu Nuwas' poem has other echoes of Hassan's – both include lines rhyming on the word *mifsali*, and Abu Nuwas' mention of wine tasting like pepper (*ka-ta'm il-fulfuli*) appears verbatim in Hassan's.

44. Wagner, *Diwan*, Book III, pp. 177–8.
45. A reference to the bubble-like shape of the Arabic letter *waw* (و), which roughly corresponds to the English 'W'.
46. Khidr is a legendary figure of wisdom traditionally held to be the unnamed 'servant' of God encountered by Moses in a story in the Qur'an (18:60–82). The narrative holds that Moses asks to accompany Khidr so as to learn from him, to which Khidr agrees on condition that Moses doesn't question anything he does. When Moses consents, Khidr then proceeds to carry out numerous seemingly destructive and wicked acts (e.g. killing a boy), each of which Moses queries with alarmed incredulity, thus violating his agreement. In the end, Khidr provides ostensible justifications for each act (e.g. the boy was a disbeliever, and thus a burden on his devout parents). Beyond the Qur'an, further tales of Khidr are found throughout Islamic (especially Sufi) theology. As it happens, the story of Khidr appears in the Qur'an immediately prior to that of Dhul-Qarnayn (see following note).
47. Dhul-Qarnayn ('He of the two horns') is a figure mentioned in a story in the Qur'an (18:83–98), in which he builds an impassable iron barrier to protect an unnamed people from the tyrannical Gog and Magog. He is thought to be based on Alexander the Great, about whom an almost identical story is told.
48. Wagner, *Diwan*, Book III, pp. 148–9.
49. The Banu Malik ('Sons of Malik') are a tribe of south Arabian origin. We see here another example of the poet (himself affiliated with the southern Banu Hakam tribe) playing

along with the rivalry between the northern and southern tribal confederations.

50. A sub-branch of the Azd tribe, of south Arabian origin. As the name suggests, they have long been influential in Oman – to this day, the ruling Al Sa'eed dynasty descends from the tribe.
51. An ancient Arab people of Yemeni origin whose recorded history dates back to at least the eighth century BC, when they were subjugated by the Assyrian emperor Sargon II. They are traditionally held to be the first settlers of the archaeological site of al-Hijr, now known as Mada'in Salih, in modern-day Saudi Arabia, later adorned with spectacular rock engravings by the Nabataeans, who also constructed the more famous Petra in today's Jordan. The Qur'an narrates Allah destroying the Thamud after they failed to heed the Prophet Salih's call to monotheism.
52. 'Amr ibn 'Amer (a.k.a. Muzayqiya') was ruler of the Sabaean kingdom centred around Ma'rib, in Yemen, when the famous Great Dam of Ma'rib was said to have burst in c. 550 AD. The event is popularly remembered as sparking the decline of ancient south Arabian civilisation (though modern historians are more inclined to point to the expansion of Roman and Persian power). Ibn 'Amer was, incidentally, of the Azd tribe.
53. Al-Masha'ir are the sites ritually visited by Muslim pilgrims at Mecca. We see here another example of the poet disavowing polytheism (*shirk*), the one sin to which he never admits, since the Qur'an states plainly that those who commit *shirk* will not be offered divine forgiveness (4:48).
54. Wagner, *Diwan*, Book III, pp. 130–2.
55. Non-Muslims at the time typically wore a girdle, called a *zunnar*, around their waists to distinguish themselves from Muslims.
56. Al-Isfahani writes the vintner is annoyed here at the suggestion his wine could be anything other than impressive.

57. Wagner, *Diwan*, Book III, pp. 126–9.
58. Among the poet's most famous lines, frequently quoted as an archetypal example of his flamboyantly scandalous, showboating persona. There evidently was a practice in some places at the time of serving drink discreetly or in disguise in public. The line appears to have got Abu Nuwas in some sort of official trouble. Al-Isfahani (citing the ninth-century grammarian al-Mubarrad) tells a story that the influential vizier of both Harun and then his son, al-Amin, al-Fadhl ibn al-Rabee', who had a low opinion of Abu Nuwas, used this line to get the poet jailed by al-Amin, leading the caliph to believe it had aroused public disapproval and thus weakened his political position vis-à-vis his brother al-Ma'mun.

    A less plausible, if more entertaining story recounted by al-Qayrawani (op. cit., p. 229) goes that Abu Nuwas was summoned before al-Amin to be executed for the line. Hearing the caliph repeat the words to him, Abu Nuwas asked, 'Well, Commander of the Believers, did he pour me [the wine]?' Al-Amin replied, 'I assume so'. To which Abu Nuwas said, 'Will you kill me over an assumption, when Allah, Mighty and Sublime, has said, "Verily, some assumptions are sinful" [49:12]?' The amused caliph ordered his guards to release the poet.
59. That is, at the very end of a summer's night, just before sunrise. Altair, which name derives directly from Arabic (*Al-Nasr al-Ta'ir*; 'The Flying Eagle'), is the brightest star in the Aquila constellation, mentioned also in WINE AND WOE. Altair disappears late at night in summer, while the Gemini constellation becomes visible shortly before dawn.
60. Implying he's attractive to both straight and gay men, on account of his epicene looks. Alternatively, 'he' may in fact be a *ghulamiyya*; that is, a girl groomed and dressed to look like a boy. Compare CEASE YOUR REPROACH; I'M NOT ONE WHO SHUNS PLEASURE.

61. 'Dragging sin's hems' has the approximate meaning of 'indulging in' sin. His choice of word for 'boastfully' may be a nod at Qur'an 31:18: 'Verily, God does not like the conceited and boastful'. There would be a ribald comedy to this – by his own admission, the men are committing acts of heinous impiety, but at least they may not be accused of pride. Montgomery reads the Arabic *fakhr* here in the traditional literary sense of a poet's boast of personal or tribal superiority, translating the ending as 'and that is no vaunt!' (op. cit., p. 133).
62. Wagner, *Diwan*, Book III, pp. 228–33.
63. Meaning the 'guard' of a vineyard, according to Ibn al-Mu'tazz (*Tabaqat al-Shu'ra'*, p. 215).
64. That is, a noon in the peak of summer. Sirius (also known in English as Alhabor, from Arabic *al-'Aboor*; the word used here), the brightest star in the night sky, happens to become visible at sunrise around the time of the summer solstice; for this reason its appearance has been regarded since ancient times as a harbinger of uncomfortable heat. Homer writes in the Iliad of it as 'an evil portent, bringing heat/ And fevers to suffering humanity' (Stanley F. Lombardo translation). The term 'dog days' derives from a Greek name for the star, 'Orion's Dog'.
65. Literally above a *mabrak*, a designated place for camels to kneel down, and a *maqeel*, a place for midday naps. The poet means the amount of shade was no larger than the width of an ostrich.
66. The Arabic in this hemistich is open to several interpretations, depending, for one thing, on diacritics. A marginal note in the Köprülü Library (Istanbul) manuscript of al-Suli's recension takes the last two words as *darrata al-saba*, translating them as 'rainwater extracted from the clouds by the *saba* [easterly] wind'. What the poet means, according to this note, is, 'I mixed the yellow [wine] with this rainwater

and poured for my friends in the tent'. The author of the note acknowledges that others have taken the words as *dirrata al-siba*, which would translate to something like 'the milk of youthful passion', but appears unconvinced by this reading.

67. A marginal note in the Ahmed Paşa Library (Istanbul) manuscript of al-Suli's recension comments: 'The beneficence of drunkenness is that he who does harm while drunk is excused'.
68. A line by the Umayyad poet Kuthayyir 'Azza (d. 723), from Medina.
69. A line also attributed to the Umayyad and 'Abbasid poet Bashar ibn Burd (d. c. 784).
70. A fifth is the amount religiously mandated as war spoils (Arabic *ghaneema* or *anfal*) from a conquered enemy. The Qur'an has an entire chapter called Al-Anfal, in which it says: 'And know that, of whatever you take as war booty, one fifth is for Allah, and the Messenger, and for close relatives, and the orphans, and the needy, and the traveller' (8:41).
71. A marginal note in the Biblioteca Ambrosiana (Milan) manuscript of the al-Suli recension reads: '[There is a saying] in the Hadith: "What an aid money is in loving God"'.
72. In other words, is it not better for 'God's fifth' to be spent generously than hoarded by a miser? Kennedy is probably right to associate the 'miser' here with the classic sanctimonious wine-abstainer and reproacher that is the target of so many of the poet's lampoons. In several poems, meanness is explicitly contrasted with bacchic conviviality (e.g., WHAT A WEAPON WINE IS; DEATH BY DRUNKENNESS; O, DAUGHTER OF THE SHEIKH, POUR FOR US). As elsewhere, Abu Nuwas mischievously implies in conclusion that drinkers are not only more virtuous than abstainers, but more pious to boot (see, e.g., WINE AND WAR, WE HAVE, IN THIS LIFE, HEAVEN'S WINE; I DRINK WINE).

V

'You, Finest Company a Drinker Could Keep'

1. Wagner, *Diwan*, Book III, pp. 26–8.
2. Meaning he prays all post-meridiem prayers at noon. Compare A CLERIC'S FATWA.
3. Numerous sources, including the poet's personal friend Abu Hiffan (see below) agree this refers to the Caliph Muhammad al-Amin, for whom the entire poem is thus a debauched form of panegyric. Strangely, however, al-Isfahani asserts the 'Muhammad' in question is a Muhammad ibn Nasr, while adding that a Muhammad ibn Mansur al-Sayrafi has also been named by others as the addressee.
4. A dirham (from Greek *drachma*) was 'a thin silver coin slightly over 2 centimetres in diameter and weighing about 3 grams' (Kennedy, H., *The Court of the Caliphs*, p. xxv). At current prices a thousand dirhams would be worth around £1,200.
5. Wagner, *Diwan*, Book I, pp. 138–9.
6. An ancient Iraqi town on the Euphrates, northwest of Baghdad, in what is today Anbar Province. 'The Arabs associated it with wine', writes Yaqut al-Hamawi in his thirteenth-century *Mu'jam al-Buldan* ('Encyclopaedia of Countries').
7. That is, those slow in passing it around to their fellow drinkers.
8. That is, the Caliph Muhammad al-Amin. The poet's use of the word *imam* may have been a dig at al-Ma'mun, who, as discussed (cf. I'M NOT ONE WHO SHUNS PLEASURE), claimed the true *imam* of the age was not al-Amin but himself.
9. Al-Amin was the sixth 'Abbasid caliph.
10. That is, the full moons – typically associated with facial beauty – weep in admiration at his smile, while swords cackle upon his displeasure, knowing the heads of his enemies shall roll.
11. Wagner, *Diwan*, Book I, pp. 236–7.
12. That is, those sitting at the drinking gathering.

13. The poet here addresses al-'Abbas ibn al-Fadhl ibn al-Rabee' – son of the veteran government administrator al-Fadhl ibn al-Rabee', vizier of both Harun and al-Amin – for whom this poem is effectively a panegyric (and is formally classified as such in Wagner's *Diwan*). The 'glower' reference plays on the literal meaning of the name 'Abbas; 'one who frowns intensely'.
14. He means to praise the generosity of al-'Abbas, who doesn't frown at the prospect of giving to others, but rather at the thought of their suffering.
15. 'Al-Fadhl' is the name of al-'Abbas' father, while, somewhat confusingly, 'Abul-Fadhl' ('The Father of Fadhl') is also a patronymic (*kunya*) of al-'Abbas'. It was, and remains, common in the Arab world to name sons after their paternal grandfathers. Again, the poet here plays on words, for one meaning of the Arabic *fadhl* is 'precedence'.
16. Wagner, *Diwan*, Book III, pp. 60–1.
17. Referring to the effaced 'traces' (*atlal*, or *dimna* in this case) in the desert sand of a former lover's campsite. The first three lines here are an example of the poet ridiculing (as discussed in the introduction) the traditional topos of weeping at the *atlal* (see also I WEPT FOR THE WINE; DON'T DRINK WITHOUT MUSIC; SAY TO WHOMEVER WEEPS FOR A VANISHED ABODE; POUR ME WHAT'S FORBIDDEN BEFORE WHAT'S PERMITTED).
18. Two towns on the Euphrates in what is today western Iraq, evidently known for wine in the poet's day.
19. That is, the Aries and Pisces sectors of the solar ecliptic, roughly corresponding to the eponymous constellations. The poet alludes here to springtime (Pisces and Aries, which occur consecutively, run from 19 February to 19 April combined). The Arabic names – *kabsh* and *hoot*, respectively – are direct translations of their Greek counterparts ('ram' and 'fish' in English) – translations, incidentally, that were probably carried out for the first time during Abu Nuwas' life. Hitti writes that while Ptolemy's Almagest (whose English

name derives from Arabic) may have been first translated during the Caliph al-Mansur's era (754–775), by the prolific translator Abu Yahya ibn al-Batriq, the more likely 'first attempt' was in Harun's day, though 'the result was not satisfactory'. The superior version, carried out by al-Hajjaj, was not completed until more than a decade after Abu Nuwas' death. It was all, in other words, cutting-edge astronomy for its time, suggesting the poet had an interest in scientific affairs (see also DO YOU NOT SEE THE SUN HAS ENTERED ARIES; WINE AND WOE; AND THE DOCTOR'S PRESCRIPTION).

20. More literally, 'When the requisite units of time have elapsed'. A marginal note in the Köprülü Library (Istanbul) manuscript of al-Suli's recension says that the 'units of time' (*al-mawaqeet*) equal fourteen days – that is, half way through a lunar month, when the full moon occurs.
21. A reference to al-'Abbas ibn al-Fadhl ibn al-Rabee' (see HE SIPPED IT WITH THE SIPPER), or to al-'Abbas ibn 'Abd Allah ibn Ja'far ibn Abi Ja'far al-Mansur, a grandson of al-Mansur's with whom the poet was friendly, or even to 'Abbas ibn 'Abd al-Muttalib, uncle of the Prophet and ostensible ancestor of the eponymous 'Abbasid dynasty.
22. A note in the Köprülü Library (Istanbul) manuscript of al-Suli's recension says: 'Meaning [pearl] white of face and [ruby] red of cheek'.
23. Wagner, *Diwan*, Book III, p. 26.
24. Wagner, *Diwan*, Book III, p. 331.
25. That is, if he chose to trace his origins. We see once again here the rivalry between northern and southern tribal confederations with which the poet, affiliated with the southerners, played along (see also YOUR REPROACH COMES FROM ENVY; ANUSHIRVAN'S HERITAGE; MANY A VINTNER I'VE COME TO, UNGUIDED).
26. Philip Kennedy writes (*The Wine Song*, p. 117) of the subtly irreligious satire at play in this line. Whereas the pious held

up faith and probity as the sole 'safeguard against the caprice of Time', Abu Nuwas instead mischievously suggests that sinful wine and pleasure-seeking are in fact the superior refuge. In this, he is (as often) more in line with the mores of the pre-Islamic poets than those of his Muslim contemporaries.

27. That is, of the riding animal. Akin to letting go of one's inhibitions; cf. DEFY THOSE, IGNORANT OF LOVE, WHO BERATE.
28. The Arabic here (*natruda 'anna 'asakir al-hazan*) has ironic echoes of Qur'an 35:34's 'Praise to Allah, who has removed from us [all] sorrow' (*al-hamdu lillah illadhi adhhaba 'anna al-hazan*).
29. That is, the 'traces' (*atlal*, or *diman* in this case) of former lovers' abandoned campsites. Here the poet blends his customary mockery of the *atlal* motif with another running joke; that of poems ending with a character drunkenly singing a line of poetry. The line in question here is attributed to the 'Abbasid poet 'Ali ibn Umayya.
30. Wagner, *Diwan*, Book III, pp. 257–8.
31. That is, the effaced 'traces' (*atlal*, or, in this case, *tulool*) in the desert sand of a former lover's campsite. This is another example of the poet ridiculing (as discussed in the introduction) the traditional topos of weeping at the *atlal*.
32. Describing a wine as 'clear as a rooster's eye' was common in classical Arabic poetry. 'Atwi writes, 'The first to [use the simile] in his poetry was the [pre-Islamic] 'Adi ibn Zayd' (*Diwan*, p. 203).
33. There is a pun here – the word for 'enmity' (*ghaleel*) can also mean 'severe thirst'.
34. A line from a poem by the pre-Islamic warrior and poet 'Adi ibn Rabee'a, a.k.a. Abu Layla al-Muhalhil ('He Who Weaves [Poetry] Finely'). 'Debris' here is the same word as the earlier 'remains' (*tulool*).
35. Wagner, *Diwan*, Book III, pp. 163–4.

36. Presumably alluding to Friday being the holy day; implying the wine offers relief from the obligations of piety.
37. Sulayman ibn Ja'far ibn Abi Ja'far al-Mansur, nicknamed Abu Ayyub, is described by Sidqi as the poet's 'worst enemy' (*Qissat Hayatihi*, p. 162), responsible for landing him in jail on more than one occasion – hence the lampoon here.
38. As discussed in the introduction, a distinction was made at the time between a weaker drink, *nabeedh*, permitted by some theologians, and the more powerful *khamr* (or, in this particular line, *rah*), which was almost universally proscribed. Today *nabeedh* is a standard word for wine of all kinds. See also GIVE BACK MY GLASS; A CLERIC'S FATWA.

VI

'I Ran with Youthful Passion Like a Wild Horse'

1. Wagner, *Diwan*, Book III, p. 153.
2. That is, the effaced 'remains' or traces (*atlal*) in the desert sand of a former lover's campsite.
3. That is, the Caliph al-Amin. As mentioned in the introduction, the caliph at one point compelled the poet to stop mocking the *atlal* motif and start incorporating it reverently into his poetry.
4. An honorific title of caliphs (more literally 'Commander of the Believers').
5. Wagner, *Diwan*, Book III, pp. 273–4.
6. That is, the Caliph al-Amin.
7. More literally, 'I am not its [drinking] companion except in conversation'. There is a possible pun, for the word for 'conversation' is *hadeeth*, meaning the line can also be read ironically as, 'I am only a [drinks] companion of the Hadith'.
8. The *tahkeem* was the slogan – *La hukma illa lillah* ('No rule except for God's') – of the Khawarij (lit. 'Departers'), an ultra-fundamentalist splinter sect. Abu Nuwas uses the Arabic word *qa'adi* (from the root *qa'da*, to sit), meaning a partisan

of the Khawarij who was unable or unwilling to fight militarily for the cause. The joke is that he, like the *qa'adi*, supports the caliph's enemies (wine, in his case) only passively, without acting on the conviction.

9. Wagner, *Diwan*, Book III, pp. 210–11.
10. These, according to Abu Hiffan, are the same Dufafa [sic] al-'Ansi and Abul-Khayr mentioned in connection with the previous poem, I DON'T TASTE THE WINE EXCEPT BY NOSE.
11. Arabic *'iyafah*, a practice dating to pre-Islamic times of divining omens by releasing birds and observing the direction of their flight. A bird that flew to the right spelled good fortune; the opposite if it flew to the left.
12. That is, fearing punishment in the hereafter, or hoping for reward. As in other poems, the poet plays on the theological contradistinction between hope (*raja'*) and fear (*khawf*, or, in this case, *makhafa*) – see also GIVE BACK MY GLASS and WILL YOU TURN PIOUS AFTER THE HAJJ?
13. Literally 'the Hadiths of Khurafa', i.e., the alleged sayings or actions of the Prophet as told by Khurafa. Tradition holds Khurafa was a man of the Banu 'Udhra tribe who became possessed by a *jinn* [spirit] which caused him to fabricate Hadiths. Thus the expression 'Hadith of Khurafa' came to be used in general for any Hadith deemed unsubstantiated. The joke here is the insinuation that the Hadiths forbidding alcohol consumption are spurious (compare I WEPT FOR THE WINE).
14. A reference to the destructive civil war fought between Harun's sons following his death in 809. As discussed in the introduction, the 'Abbasid empire as a whole never fully regained its power and territorial reach after the war.
15. Wagner, *Diwan*, Book III, pp. 41–3.
16. A marginal note in the Köprülü Library (Istanbul) manuscript of al-Suli's recension reads: 'Al-Amin had forbidden Abu Nuwas from drinking when he learned al-Ma'mun was

ordering the preachers in Khorasan to disgrace al-Amin with Abu Nuwas' poetry'.

17. An honorific title of caliphs.
18. Meaning a beam of light extending as a long tent rope (*tunub*) does from the ground to the canopy.
19. A note in the Köprülü Library (Istanbul) manuscript of al-Suli's recension reads: 'That is, he made an appointment to see me with a wink from his eye'.
20. Wagner, *Diwan*, Book III, pp. 334–6.
21. 'From Greek-Latin *denarius*; the unit of gold currency in the caliphate, weighing about 4 grams' (Hitti, op. cit., p. 171). At today's prices, 80 dinars of 24kt gold would be worth almost £10,000.
22. 'The Son of Amram', i.e. Moses, meaning the vintner was Jewish.
23. The poet's register here turns Islamic, recalling the Qur'anic concepts of 'hardship' (*'usr*) and 'ease' (*yusr*), from which roots the words 'impoverished' (*mu'sir*) and 'rich' (*musir*) in this case derive.
24. Literally 'Once the wine clothed me in Hunain's sandals'. To be 'clothed in Hunain's sandals' is to be rendered empty-handed. An Arabic folk tale goes that there was once a renowned shoemaker in al-Hira named Hunain. One day a Bedouin came on camel to his shop and asked the price of a pair of shoes he liked. A lengthy negotiation ensued over the price, finally culminating after several hours of exhaustive back-and-forth in agreement, at which point the Bedouin abruptly decided he no longer wished to buy the sandals, and left. A furious Hunain, who had lost not only precious time but customers – indeed, hadn't sold a thing all day on account of the Bedouin – decided to exact revenge. Riding in the direction the Bedouin had gone, but taking a shortcut to get ahead of him, he placed one of the sandals on the ground, then the other some distance ahead of it, and then hid. Seeing first the one shoe, then the other, and

thinking to himself how alike they were to the ones in Hunain's shop, the Bedouin dismounted at the second and walked to get the first. At this point Hunain, who had been watching, hopped onto the Bedouin's camel and fled with it. Thus the Bedouin was forced to walk the several miles back to his campsite, destitute but for Hunain's sandals.

25. Wagner, *Diwan*, Book I, pp. 122–5.
26. That is, the effaced 'traces' (*atlal*) in the desert sand of a former lover's campsite. Unusually for the poet, he adopts the *atlal* topos reverently and unironically here, in contrast to his customary ridicule of it (see introduction). This may be explained by the formality of the occasion, not least because Harun – to whom this is addressed as a panegyric – was known to be no fan of Abu Nuwas' flippancy in general.
27. Alluding to intense frustration.
28. Because they're used to late-night visitors; compare HOW MANY A TAVERN-KEEPER I'VE FRIGHTENED.
29. Meaning rays of sunlight breaking through gaps in a cloudy sky, according to a marginal note in the Köprülü Library (Istanbul) manuscript of al-Suli's recension.
30. More literally his 'sword-belts'. The poet means to praise the caliph's height; to call someone 'long of sword-belt' is to say they are tall.
31. A dirham (from Greek *drachma*) was 'a thin silver coin slightly over 2 centimetres in diameter and weighing about 3 grams' (Kennedy, H., *The Court of the Caliphs*, p. xxv). At current prices twenty thousand dirhams would be worth over £23,000.
32. Al-Amin (real name Muhammad) was given his regal title in 791 or 792, while al-Ma'mun (born 'Abd Allah) was not given his until 798 or 799. A formal succession pact announced in 802 also designated another son, al-Mu'tamin, to be third in line to the throne. It would thus have made little sense to refer to Harun as '*Abu al-Umana*" before this time.

33. Wagner, *Diwan*, Book III, pp. 82–4.
34. The opening line of a poem by Jareer (d. 758), a celebrated poet from Najd, in what is today Saudi Arabia. Dhu Tuloohi was a site in Najd where, according to pre-Islamic folklore, a battle was fought between the Bakr and Tameem tribes (cf. ANUSHIRVAN'S HERITAGE) after a dispute over a woman. The line suggests (as do others, e.g., in RAMADAN'S FAST FORBADE US WINE) that song recitals of old poetry were a feature of drinking sessions.
35. An Arabian gazelle. Abu Dhabi, the capital of the United Arab Emirates, means 'The Father of the *Dhabi*'. Abu Nuwas intends it here as a metaphor for a handsome youth.
36. Wagner, *Diwan*, Book III, pp. 233–6.
37. That is, heartache.
38. Meaning, as a note in the Ahmed Paşa Library (Istanbul) manuscript of al-Suli's recension explains, that he would sleep with married women.
39. Though early Arabic writing, including in the initial period after Islam, did not contain dots, they were later added to distinguish between letters that would otherwise look identical (e.g. ت، ث، ن، ب). 'Vowelling' (Arabic *tashkeel*) is the use of diacritical marks above and below letters to signify short vowels, gemination, silences, and other distinctions.
40. Wagner, *Diwan*, Book III, pp. 208–9.
41. More precisely, with jet-black irises starkly contrasted with bright white sclerae – regarded as a feature of beauty.
42. That is, pronouncing it gutturally, as in French. Abu Nuwas was himself said to have the same rhotacism.
43. I.e., owing to the bulk of his behind.
44. Wagner, *Diwan*, Book III, pp. 29–35.
45. The 'Mirbad of Basra', according to Yaqut al-Hamawi's thirteenth-century *Mu'jam al-Buldan* ('Encyclopaedia of Countries'), was 'one of [Basra's] most famous places'; originally a camel market (the literal meaning of *mirbad*),

later a built-up quarter frequented by poets, who would congregate there to recite verses. Why Abu Nuwas – who, of course, lived in Basra in his youth – speaks of 'the two Mirbads' (*al-mirbadan*) is unclear. Of 'al-Labab', al-Hamawi says simply it is 'a place', quoting a few lines by the poet Ibn al-A'rabi mentioning it.

46. It's possible that the words for 'courts' (*al-rahab*) and 'lobbies' (*al-sihan*) are in fact place-names of other sites in Basra; al-Hamawi, however, makes no mention of any such locales.
47. The 'brother' lost here is Basra, from which he subsequently cut himself off entirely. The next line marks his move to Baghdad in the late 780s.
48. Surely a significant line given his real mother's abandonment of him in childhood. See also CLOUDS OF WOE.
49. That is, the grapevine.
50. That is, the poet's and the doves'.
51. Referring to spider webs, according to both al-Isfahani and a note in the al-Thahiriyya Library (Damascus) manuscript of al-Suli's recension.
52. More literally, 'By a clumsy seamstress, for whom no cord nor tent rope was fastened to the ground'. A note in the Köprülü Library (Istanbul) manuscript of al-Suli's recension clarifies this means it was woven 'without [proper] weaving apparatus' – because, again, the 'weaver' is in fact a spider.
53. I.e., the wine is so golden as to be indistinguishable from the gold vessel.
54. Al-Isfahani says this is because the vessels belong to Christians; i.e., the setting is a monastery or some other Christian-owned tavern. Sidqi calls the vessels 'Byzantine' (*Alhan al-Han*, p. 249).
55. That is, the wine's bubbles.
56. Wagner, *Diwan*, Book III, p. 265.
57. Seemingly the same place now known as Firzol in today's Lebanon. In his thirteenth-century *Mu'jam al-Buldan*

('Encyclopaedia of Countries'), the author Yaqut al-Hamawi mentions an 'al-Farzal' as a village 'of the Biqaʿ of Baʿlabakk [...] at the feet of her western mountain'. Modern Firzol is indeed located in the Biqaʿ Valley, at the feet of Mount Lebanon, about 30km southwest of Baʿlabakk (now more commonly pronounced Baʿalbak). Though al-Hamawi doesn't mention any association with wine, he does say al-Farzal [sic] is known for raisins, suggesting grapes were also grown. In general, the highly fertile soil of the Biqaʿ, naturally irrigated by snowy mountains on two sides, has been a winemaking region for millennia. Baʿalbak's famous Roman ruins contain a magnificently well-preserved temple consecrated to the wine god Bacchus, and the ode (*muʿallaqa*) of the sixth-century pre-Islamic poet ʿAmr ibn Kulthum (killed, legend has it, by an undiluted wine binge) mentions drinking 'many a glass' in the town. In 1857, Jesuit priests founded the modern Lebanese wine industry at Ksara, just 7km from Firzol. The author can attest from experience to the quality of Firzol's *ʿaraq*, a grape and aniseed distillate akin to French pastis, Greek ouzo, Turkish raki, etc.

VII
'Pour for Us, for Today is Ram Day'

1. Wagner, *Diwan*, Book III, pp. 356–7.
2. Meaning Jibreel ibn Bukhtishuʿ, a Christian doctor of Harun's, who went by the patronymic Abu ʿIsa (al-Qayrawani, op. cit., p. 237). As mentioned in the introduction, many eminent physicians of the time were perfectly serious in their view that wine offered medical benefits (as indeed many are today). The notion here of a doctor recommending wine to a patient, then, need not by any means be thought wholly frivolous or parodic.
3. Sidqi writes that these 'four natures' were heat, coldness, wetness, and dryness; a notion that was 'current in [the poet's]

time' (*Qissat Hayatihi*, p. 59). Indeed, this was the so-called 'humoral' hypothesis of Hippocrates and Galen, whose works had long been known (whether in the original Greek or in Syriac translation) to the Nestorian Christian physicians of Iraq – such as Jibreel ibn Bukhtishu' (Cooperson, *Al-Ma'mun*, pp. 91–2). The above poem is thus a front-row seat at the transmission of ancient Greek thought into 'Abbasid science – and another example of Abu Nuwas' fascination with this process, which had only begun within his lifetime (c.f. DO YOU NOT SEE THE SUN HAS ENTERED ARIES; WINE AND WOE; and ANBAR WINE).

4. Wagner, *Diwan*, Book III, pp. 157–9.
5. Of camels, specifically (Arabic *hajma*). As will be seen, this is meant metaphorically.
6. As al-Isfahani comments, the 'flock' here refers to dark red grapes, while the green 'fur' is the vine leaves.
7. A canal linking the Euphrates to the Tigris at Baghdad.
8. Places in or around Baghdad renowned at the time for their wine.
9. Sixth-century king of the Sassanid Empire, the last Persian empire before the rise of Islam. Its capital was at Ctesiphon, around 35km south of where Baghdad would later be built. Anushirvan is largely remembered as a moderniser and patron of philosophy and learning, particularly that of the Greeks and Indians. Under the Zoroastrian Sassanids, wine was freely and widely consumed, and indeed much revered.
10. Tameem and Bakr are among the most famous of the northern Arab tribes, hailing from the Najd desert in today's Saudi Arabia. We see again here the southern versus northern Arab rivalry with which the poet, affiliated with the southerners, played along (see also YOUR REPROACH COMES FROM ENVY; MANY A VINTNER I'VE COME TO, UNGUIDED; A SAFEGUARD AGAINST THE CAPRICE OF TIME).
11. Wagner, *Diwan*, Book III, pp. 271–3.

12. 'Ram Day' is the twenty-first day of every Persian month. 'It's a day on which [the Persians] enjoy pleasure and make merry, as they do on Bahram, which is the twentieth day', reads a note in the Ahmed Paşa Library (Istanbul) manuscript of al-Suli's recension.
13. *Calendula officinalis*, to be precise; also known as English marigold. The poet uses the word *adhariyoon*, an Arabisation of the Persian name (meaning 'colour of fire').
14. Wagner, *Diwan*, Book III, pp. 242–5.
15. The poet alludes here to the Persian New Year, Nowruz, which begins with the vernal equinox (usually 21 March), when the sun reaches the First Point of Aries, so-named by the Greek astronomer Hipparchus because, at the time (second century BC), it occurred when the sun first met, or 'entered', the Aries constellation. Because the orientation of the earth's axis itself is inconstant (a phenomenon called axial precession), the First Point of Aries changes over time, and is today located in Pisces. Heralding the advent of spring, Nowruz was and still is a major Persian festival, and the holiest day in Zoroastrianism. Abu Nuwas' celebration of it here is of a piece with his general enthusiasm for Persian culture. Incidentally, the Arabic for Aries, *hamal*, is a direct translation of the Greek (English 'ram') – a translation that was probably carried out for the first time during Abu Nuwas' life. Hitti writes that Ptolemy's Almagest (whose English name derives from the Arabic) may have been first translated during the Caliph al-Mansur's era (754–775), by the prolific translator Abu Yahya ibn al-Batriq, although the more likely 'first attempt' was in Harun al-Rashid's day, 'the result [of which] was not satisfactory'. The superior version, carried out by Al-Hajjaj, was not completed until more than a decade after Abu Nuwas' death. This was all, in other words, cutting-edge astronomy in the poet's day, suggesting he had an interest in scientific affairs (see also ANBAR WINE; WINE AND WOE; and THE DOCTOR'S PRESCRIPTION).

16. Referring to the almost exact parity in the length of day and night on the vernal equinox, due to the plane of the earth's equator aligning with the centre of the sun (the word 'equinox' comes from Latin *aequinoctium*; 'the time of equal days and nights').
17. In a lengthy note, Al-Isfahani writes about the multiple interpretations of this line by various literary commentators. The ambiguity derives from the word *hawl*, which has several distinct meanings, including 'a full year', 'power', and 'transformation'. Thus the line can be read 'And the wine has completed its full year' (the interpretation of Muhammad ibn Yahya al-Thaqafi); or 'And the wine has undergone its full transformation' (the view of Ahmad ibn Yahya al-Shaybani, a.k.a. Tha'lab); or 'And the wine has acquired its full power' (as argued by al-Mubarrad). The 'full year' interpretation would seem to make little sense, as grapes are harvested after the summer, meaning the wine would not have aged a full year by the start of spring. Even if one supposes he means the wine began its life with the breaking open of the grape buds in the spring of the previous year, it would be wholly out of character for Abu Nuwas to extol so young a wine. The double/triple entendre may well have been deliberate; in any case, I have aimed above for a translation broad enough to accommodate the three possibilities.
18. Wagner, *Diwan*, Book III, pp. 28–9.
19. That is, the mixture must be just right. Compare PRAISE THE BLESSINGS OF THIS WINE.
20. According to al-Isfahani, this poem was composed during the 811–813 civil war between the Caliph al-Amin's forces in Baghdad and those of his half-brother, al-Ma'mun, who would ultimately topple him after invading from the eastern province of Khorasan. The story, as told by al-Isfahani, goes that an Ibrahim al-Tabari was sitting by his front door during the war when Abu Nuwas passed by. When al-Tabari asked

the poet about the latest news from the frontlines, he replied, 'I don't have any, but let's you and I go make some news!' The pair then went for a drink in a garden, and when someone later approached them to recount reports of the day's various battlefield victories and defeats, Abu Nuwas quickly cut him off and began reciting the above poem.

21. The 'good deeds' (*khayrat*) are mentioned several times in the Qur'an, where praise is given to those who 'hasten' to them (see e.g. 3:114; 21:90; 23:61). The joke here, as so often, is that drinking is a 'good deed', i.e., a pious one (see also THE HILLTOP TENT; WE HAVE, IN THIS LIFE, HEAVEN'S WINE; I DRINK WINE).
22. Wagner, *Diwan*, Book V, pp. 174–5.
23. As noted in the introduction, this verse constitutes an example of what might be termed Abu Nuwas' anti-war poetry. The mention of 'mangonels' suggests it may have been composed during the 812–3 siege of Baghdad by al-Ma'mun's forces.
24. Wagner, *Diwan*, Book V, p. 175.
25. The name of a friend of Abu Nuwas' who took up arms against the Khawarij, and tried to convince the poet to do the same, according to al-Isfahani. The latter decade of Harun's reign saw considerable Kharijite violence in the province of Khorasan.
26. Arabic *sukhub*; necklaces made from perfumed carnations.

Bibliography

Ahmed, Shahab, *What is Islam? The Importance of Being Islamic*, Princeton University Press, 2016.

Amis, Kingsley, *Everyday Drinking*, Bloomsbury, 2009.

al-'Aqqad, 'Abbas Mahmud, *Abu Nuwas: Dirasa fi al-Tahleel al-Nafsani wal-Naqd al-Tareekhi* ('Abu Nuwas: A Study in Psychological Analysis and Historical Commentary'), Nahdet Misr, 2007.

al-'Askari, Abu Hilal al-Hasan ibn 'Abd Allah, *Diwan Abi Mihjan al-Thaqafi wa Sharhuh* ('The Collected Poems of Abu Mihjan al-Thaqafi and a Commentary Thereon'), Matba'at al-Azhar al-Baruniyya, 1900.

'Atwi, 'Ali Najeeb, *Diwan Abi Nuwas: Al-Khamriyyat* ('The Collected Poems of Abu Nuwas: The Wine Odes'), Dar wa Maktabat al-Hilal, 2008.

al-Barquqi, 'Abd al-Rahman, *Sharh Diwan Hassan ibn Thabit al-Ansari* ('A Commentary on the Collected Poems of Hassan ibn Thabit al-Ansari'), Al-Matba'a al-Rahmaniyya, 1929.

Bazmee Ansari, 'Abd al-Samad, 'D̲jahāngīr', in: *Encyclopaedia of Islam, Second Edition*, P. Bearman, Th. Bianquis, C.E. Bosworth, E. van Donzel, W.P. Heinrichs (eds), Brill, 2012.

Bencheikh, Jamel-Eddine, 'K̲h̲amriyya', in: *Encyclopaedia of Islam, Second Edition*, P. Bearman, Th. Biạnquis, C.E. Bosworth, E. van Donzel, W.P. Heinrichs (eds), Brill, 2012.

Boutz, Jennifer Hill, 'Ḥassān Ibn Thābit, A True *Mukhaḍram*: A Study of the Ghassānid Odes of Ḥassān Ibn Thābit', Ph.D. dissertation, Georgetown University, 2009.

Burns, Robert, *A Choice of Burns's Poems and Songs*, Faber and Faber, 1966.

Cooperson, Michael, 'al-Amīn, Muḥammad', in: *Encyclopaedia of Islam, Third Edition*, Kate Fleet, Gudrun Krämer, Denis Matringe, John Nawas, Everett Rowson (eds), Brill, 2010.

——— *Al-Ma'mun*, Oneworld Publications, 2005.

Dunlop, Douglas Morton, 'al-Balkhī', in: *Encyclopaedia of Islam, Second Edition*, P. Bearman, Th. Bianquis, C.E. Bosworth, E. van Donzel, W.P. Heinrichs (eds), Brill, 2012.

Fouchécour, Ch.-H. De and Rosenfeld, B.A., ''Umar Khayyam', in: *Encyclopaedia of Islam, Second Edition*, P. Bearman, Th. Bianquis, C.E. Bosworth, E. van Donzel, W.P. Heinrichs (eds), Brill, 2012.

Gabrieli, Francesco, *Diwan al-Walid ibn Yazid al-Umawi* ['The Collected Poems of al-Walid ibn Yazid the Umayyad'], Dar al-Kitab al-Jadeed (Beirut), 1967.

Gimaret, Daniel, 'Mu'tazila', in: *Encyclopaedia of Islam, Second Edition*, P. Bearman, Th. Bianquis, C.E. Bosworth, E. van Donzel, W.P. Heinrichs (eds), Brill, 2012.

Groot, Alexander H. de, 'Murād IV', in: *Encyclopaedia of Islam, Second Edition*, P. Bearman, Th. Bianquis, C.E. Bosworth, E. van Donzel, W.P. Heinrichs (eds), Brill, 2012.

al-Hamawi, Yaqut, *Mu'jam al-Buldan* ('Encyclopaedia of Countries'), Dar Sader, 1993.

Hamori, Andras, 'Examples of Convention in the Poetry of Abū Nuwās', *Studia Islamica*, No. 30 (1969), pp. 5–26.

——— *On the Art of Medieval Arabic Literature*, Princeton University Press, 1974.

Heine, Peter, 'Nabīdh', in: *Encyclopaedia of Islam, Second Edition*, P. Bearman, Th. Bianquis, C.E. Bosworth, E. van Donzel, W.P. Heinrichs (eds), Brill, 2012.

el-Hibri, Tayeb, 'Harun al-Rashid and the Mecca Protocol of 802: A Plan for Division or Succession?', *International Journal of Middle East Studies*, Vol. 24, No. 3 (Aug. 1992), pp. 461–480.

Hitti, Philip K., *History of the Arabs: From the Earliest Times to the Present*, Revised tenth edition, Palgrave Macmillan, 2002.

Housman, Alfred Edward, *A Shropshire Lad and Other Poems*, Penguin Classics, 2010.

Hussein, Taha, *Khisam wa Naqd* ('Argument and Criticism'), Hindawi Foundation for Education and Culture, 2014.

Ibn Manthur, *Abu Nuwas: Fi Tareekhihi wa Shi'rihi wa Mabadhilihi wa 'Abathihi wa Mujoonih* ('Abu Nuwas: On His History, Poetry, Private Life, Levity, and Ribaldry'), 'Umar Abu al-Nasr (ed.), Matba'at al-Najwa, 1969.

Ingrams, William Harold, *Abu Nuwas in Life and in Legend*, privately published in Mauritius, 1933.

Judd, Steven, 'Reinterpreting al-Walīd b. Yazīd', *Journal of the American Oriental Society*, Vol. 128, No. 3 (2008), pp. 439–458.

Kennedy, Hugh, *The Court of the Caliphs: When Baghdad Ruled the Muslim World*, Phoenix, 2004.

——— *The Prophet and the Age of the Caliphates: The Islamic Near East from the Sixth to the Eleventh Century*, Second edition, Routledge, 2004.

Kennedy, Philip F., *Abu Nuwas: A Genius of Poetry*, Oneworld Publications, 2005.

——— '*Khamr* and *Ḥikma* in *Jāhilī* Poetry', *Journal of Arabic Literature*, Vol. 20, No. 2 (1989), pp. 97–114.

——— Review of *The Rhetoric of Sobriety: Wine in Early Islam* by Kathryn Kueny, *Journal of the Royal Asiatic Society*, Vol. 12, No. 3 (2002), pp. 366–70.

——— *The Wine Song in Classical Arabic Poetry: Abu Nuwas and the Literary Tradition*, Oxford University Press, 1997.

Khuraybani, Ja'far, *Abu Nuwas: Al-Hasan ibn Hani'*, Dar al-Kutub al-'Ilmiyya, 1990.

Kueny, Kathryn, *The Rhetoric of Sobriety: Wine in Early Islam*, State University of New York Press, 2001.

Levi Della Vida, Giorgio, 'Kh̲āridj̲ites', in: *Encyclopaedia of Islam, Second Edition*, P. Bearman, Th. Bianquis, C.E. Bosworth, E. van Donzel, W.P. Heinrichs (eds), Brill, 2012.

Madelung, Wilferd, 'Murdji'a', in: *Encyclopaedia of Islam, Second Edition*, P. Bearman, Th. Bianquis, C.E. Bosworth, E. van Donzel, W.P. Heinrichs (eds), Brill, 2012.

Marozzi, Justin, *Baghdad: City of Peace, City of Blood*, Penguin, 2015.

Massington, L. , Radtke, B., Chittick, W.C., Jong, F. de., Lewisohn, L., Zarcone, Th., Ernst, C, Aubin, Françoise and J.O. Hunwick, 'Taṣawwuf', in: *Encyclopaedia of Islam, Second Edition*, P. Bearman, Th. Bianquis, C.E. Bosworth, E. van Donzel, W.P. Heinrichs (eds), Brill, 2012.

al-Mihzami, Abu Hiffan ibn Harb, *Akhbar Abi Nuwas: Al-Hasan ibn Hani* ('Stories of Abu Nuwas: Al-Hasan ibn Hani'), edited by Faraj al-Hiwar, Manshurat al-Jamal, 2011.

Montgomery, James E., 'Abū Nuwās, The Justified Sinner?', *Oriens*, Vol. 39, No. 1 (2011), pp. 75–164.

——— 'For the Love of a Christian Boy: A Song by Abū Nuwās', *Journal of Arabic Literature*, Vol. 27, No. 2 (1996), pp. 115–124.

——— 'Revelry and Remorse: A Poem of Abū Nuwās', *Journal of Arabic Literature*, Vol. 25, No. 2 (1994), pp. 116–34.

al-Muqri, 'Ali, *Al-Khamr wal-Nabeedh fi al-Islam* ('Strong and Weak Wine in Islam'), Riad El-Rayyes Books, 2007.

al-Mu'tazz, Ibn, *Tabaqat al-Shu'ra'* ('The Classes of Poets'), 'Abd al-Sattar Ahmad Farraj (ed.), Dar al-Ma'arif, 1956.

Noorani, Yaseen, 'Heterotopia and the Wine Poem in Early Islamic Culture', *International Journal of Middle East Studies*, Vol. 36, No. 3 (2004), pp. 345–66.

Omar, Faruq, 'Hārūn al-Rashīd', in: *Encyclopaedia of Islam, Second Edition*, P. Bearman, Th. Bianquis, C.E. Bosworth, E. van Donzel, W.P. Heinrichs (eds), Brill, 2012.

al-Qayrawani, Ibrahim ibn al-Qasim al-Raqeeq, *Al-Mukhtar min Qutb al-Suroor fi Awsaf al-Anbidha wal-Khumoor* ('A Selection from "The Variegated Pleasures of Descriptions of Wines and Strong Drinks"'), abridged by Nur al-Din 'Ali al-Mas'udi, 'Abd al-Hafeeth Mansur (ed.), 'Abd al-Kareem ibn 'Abd Allah Establishment, 1976.

Rekaya, Mohamed, 'al-Ma'mūn', in: *Encyclopaedia of Islam, Second Edition*, P. Bearman, Th. Bianquis, C.E. Bosworth, E. van Donzel, W.P. Heinrichs (eds), Brill, 2012.

Sadan, Joseph, 'Mas͟hrūbāt', in: *Encyclopaedia of Islam, Second Edition*, P. Bearman, Th. Bianquis, C.E. Bosworth, E. van Donzel, W.P. Heinrichs (eds), Brill, 2012.

Sidqi, 'Abd al-Rahman, *Abu Nuwas: Qissat Hayatihi wa Shi'rih* ('Abu Nuwas: The Story of his Life and Poetry'), Dar Ihya' al-Kutub al-'Arabiyya, 1944.

——— *Alhan al-Han* ('The Tunes of the Tavern'), Dar al-Ma'arif, 1947.

Van Gelder, Geert Jan, 'Dubious Genres: On Some Poems by Abū Nuwās', *Arabica*, T. 44, Fasc. 2 (Apr. 1997), pp. 268–283.

Wagner, Ewald, 'Abū Nuwās', in: *Encyclopaedia of Islam, Third Edition*, Kate Fleet, Gudrun Krämer, Denis Matringe, John Nawas, Everett Rowson (eds), Brill, 2010.

——— *Diwan Abi Nuwas al-Hasan ibn Hani' al-Hakami* ('The Collected Poems of Abu Nuwas al-Hasan ibn Hani' al-Hakami'), with Gregor Schoeler, Beirut, 2015.

Wensinck, Arent Jan and Sadan, Joseph, 'K͟hamr', in: *Encyclopaedia of Islam, Second Edition*, P. Bearman, Th. Bianquis, C.E. Bosworth, E. van Donzel, W.P. Heinrichs (eds), Brill, 2012.

Wilmot, John, *Rochester: Selected Poems*, Paul Davis (ed.), Oxford World's Classics, 2013.

Index